The FREEDOM of Letting Go

BY DONNA CLARK GOODRICH

*This is the day the L*ORD *has made; let us rejoice and be glad in it.* (Psalm 118:24)

The FREEDOM of *Letting Go*

All rights reserved. The author guarantees all contents are original and do not infringe upon the legal rights of any other person or work. No part of this book may be used or reproduced, stored in a retrieval system or transmitted in any form or by any means without prior written permission of the publisher, except in the case of brief quotations embodied in critical articles and reviews.

For information, address Comfort Publishing, 296 Church St. N., Concord, NC 28025. The views expressed in this book are not necessarily those of the publisher.

Copyright ©2012 by Donna Clark Goodrich

First printing

Book cover design
by Reed Karriker

Cover photo: ©Photo_Concepts/istockphoto

ISBN: 978-1-936695-65-2
Published by Comfort Publishing, LLC
www.comfortpublishing.com

Printed in the United States of America

DEDICATION

I want to dedicate this book to:

My "more precious than gold" husband, Gary, for his godly life and the love he's shown me for more than 50 years.

Our three extra-special children: Robert, Janet, and Patty, who have always been there when we needed them (and who provided many illustrations for this book).

Our son-in-law, Ned, who gave us a good reason to let go of our daughter, Janet, and has been a great husband to her for more than 25 years.

Our two granddaughters, Heather and Lindsay, who have brought so much joy into our family.

And to my Lord and Savior, Jesus Christ, who gave me the courage and grace to let go of many things in my life and helped me to press forward.

Unless otherwise indicated, all Scripture quotations are taken from the HOLY BIBLE, NEW INTERNATIONAL VERSION®. NIV®. Copyright ©1973, 1978, 1984 by the International Bible Society. Used by permission of Zondervan. All rights reserved.

Verses marked KJV are taken from the King James version of the Bible.

Verses marked NKJV are taken from the New King James version. Copyright ©1982 by Thomas Nelson Inc. Used by permission. All rights reserved.

Verses marked NLT are taken from the Holy Bible, New Living Translation, copyright ©1996, 2004. Used by permission of Tyndale House Publishers Inc., Wheaton, IL 60189 USA. All rights reserved.

Verses marked MSG are taken from The Message. Copyright © by Eugene H. Peterson 1993, 1994, 1995, 1996, 2000, 2001, 2002. Used by permission of NavPress Publishing Group.

CONTENTS

1. LETTING GO OF GRIEF
Do you have trouble saying good-bye to a loved one — a spouse, a child, a parent, a friend? You can let go and move on.

2. LETTING GO OF FAILURES —YOUR OWN AND OTHER PEOPLE'S
Sometimes it's easier to let go of other people's failures than it is your own. You can do both.

3. LETTING GO OF YOUR SUCCESSES
Do you remind yourself and others of your successes? Are these successes in man's eyes or God's? Your talents are only on loan from God.

4. LETTING GO OF POSSESSIONS
Do you have an addiction to credit cards? Learn how to simplify your life and break the habit of craving material things to bring you happiness.

5. LETTING GO OF THE HURTS IN YOUR LIFE
Do hurtful words and actions keep spinning in your head? Do you relive the pain over and over? Put these hurts in the "forgiven" file.

6. LETTING GO OF YOUR CHILDREN
Are you experiencing the empty nest syndrome? Have your children strayed from your teachings? Let go, and leave them in God's hands.

7. LETTING GO OF HEALTH ISSUES
Is your main topic of conversation an "organ recital"? Do you worry about your family's health? Let Scripture be your guide instead of WebMD.com.

8. Letting Go of Your Youth
Do clerks offer you the senior discount ten years early? Does getting old depress you? Learn how to look in the mirror and laugh!

9. Letting Go of Guilt
Even though you know God has forgiven you, do past sins come back to haunt you? You can leave them all at the cross.

10. Letting Go of Control
Do you always have to be in charge? Does it bother you when someone else is? Accept the fact that God is in control — and He does a much better job.

11. Letting Go of Worry
If worry was an Olympic event, would you take home the gold medal? Turn your concerns over to God and relax.

12. Letting Go of Doubt
Have your family and friends nicknamed you "Thomas"? Accept God's promises and know that His foundation stands sure. (2 Timothy 2:19 KJV)

13. Letting Go of Fear
Are you fearful of tomorrow? There are three-hundred and sixty-five "fear nots" in God's Word — one for each day of the year. Select one and make it your own.

14. The Land Beyond Letting Go
Now that you've let go of the things holding you back, discover what can take their place so you can "press on toward the goal." (Philippians 3:14 NIV)

FOREWORD

In my years of crisscrossing the United States, teaching seminars and workshops on various aspects of communication, I've had the enjoyable experience of working with Donna Goodrich many times. Although I was a fellow faculty member, as often as possible I would become a student and sit in on her presentations. I knew that whatever her topic would be, she would provide valuable life lessons presented in a humorous, uplifting, positive way.

What makes Donna succeed as a public speaker, as a teacher, and as an author is the fact that she is always genuine. She shares from her heart, offering valuable life experiences in an open and kind way. Her words nurture, enlighten, entertain, reveal, and challenge. She is well read. She has traveled widely. She has met people from all walks of life, all backgrounds, all interests, and she has provided a special wisdom that has made her a favorite of all who meet her.

This latest book, *The Freedom of Letting Go,* is a compendium of knowledge gained from years of personal study, decades of hands-on experience, and a lifetime of listening and sharing. You will have your eyes opened to a vast range of material, presented by a gifted storyteller, master instructor, and deep thinker. Turn the pages and begin to grow.

Dennis E. Hensley, Ph.D.
Author, *The Power of Positive Productivity*

INTRODUCTION

We often think of letting go only when a loved one dies. However, I vividly recall the day God showed me that letting go involved every area of my life. It was on a Sunday morning, eleven years after I had lost a very special person in my life — my mother. After grieving for that extraordinary period of time, God finally gave me the strength to say good-bye to her at a church campground where our family had spent many summers.

Two weeks later, I sat in my home church listening to the sermon. Enjoying a peace in my heart that I hadn't experienced in a long time, I thought, *I need to write about this.*

An outline came to me and I began to jot down points on the back of the bulletin. The logical verses to use were Philippians 3:13-14: "This one thing I do, forgetting those things which are behind, and reaching forth unto those things which are before, I press toward the mark…" (KJV).

Then the Lord seemed to say, *Read those verses again. There's a comma between them. They go together. You can't press toward the mark unless you first forget those things which are behind.*

You do not move ahead by constantly looking in a rearview mirror. The past is a rudder to guide you, not an anchor to drag you down. We must learn from the past but not live in the past. (Warren W. Wiersbe)

In the weeks to come, as I faced various experiences, it suddenly occurred to me that I was responding differently to each one than I had in the past. I didn't get upset at unkind words. I didn't nag my husband every day about his illnesses and how he was feeling. When I disagreed with something one of our children did, something checked me before I offered criticism.

I wondered one day in my quiet time, *Is all this change because I let go of Mother?* Then I realized it wasn't just the idea of saying goodbye to my mother. It was the whole principle of letting go — letting go of the state we had left twenty-four years before, letting go of my husband's health, letting go of our married daughter and her family, and our unmarried son and daughter. It included letting go of possessions, of people who had hurt me, of wanting to have control.

When my friend and I were repacking our luggage to return home from Great Britain, she said, "I need to jettison some things." I had never heard that word before and asked her what it meant. "Get rid of things I don't need," she said. "Things I don't have room for. I need to make room for the things that are important."

We probably all have things to jettison in our lives. We need to let go of things from our past to make room for important things we need in our lives right now or in days to come. Norman Vincent Peale said, "If in addition to present problems, you pile high on your memory past actions that are now outdated, you will go staggering through life under an impossible load."[1]

The present is all we have. We must not let the pain and regrets of the past – and the uncertainties of the future — rob us of a happy and productive present. (Lyle Flinner)

The Italians have a custom on New Year's Eve. The streets clear; there is no traffic, no pedestrians, not even policemen. Then, at the stroke of midnight, the windows of the houses fly open. To the sound of laughter, music, and fireworks, each member of the family pitches out old dishes, ornaments, hated furniture, and other personal possessions that remind them of something in the past year they are determined to wipe out of their minds.[2]

A church in West Palm Beach, Florida, holds a similar event. On New Year's Eve, they hold a "burning bowl" ceremony. Church members examine their lives and write down what they'll let go of in the coming year, then they drop the notes into a burning fire in a Grecian urn.[3]

Wouldn't that be a great thing for us to do — not only at the end of every year, but at the end of every day? Do you ever go to bed at night and fret over the day's activities? Do you worry over something you said or did that you shouldn't have, or wonder if a decision you made was the right one?

That was the case with a businessman who was always doubtful as to whether he had done or said the right thing. Finally, he broke the habit by tearing off the calendar page for that day, rolling it into a ball and dropping that "day" into the wastebasket. Then he prayed: "Lord, You gave me this day. I did the best I could with it and You helped me, and I thank You. I made some mistakes. That was when I didn't follow Your advice, and I am sorry about that. Forgive me. But I had some successes, too, and I am grateful for Your guidance. But now, Lord, mistakes or successes, the day is over and I'm through with it, so I'm giving it back to You. Amen."[4]

Letting go of the past gives us release. Author and speaker, Betty Arthurs, demonstrates this in a talk based on Luke 7:36-50:

> Reality of God's forgiveness
> Expression of love
> Leave your guilt
> Enter peaceful place
> Assurance of forgiveness
> Serve others
> Escape your past

It is my prayer that as you read this book, God will give you strength for whatever you may be going through today. And I pray that as you read, you too will discover *The Freedom of Letting Go*.

To let go doesn't mean to stop caring,
it means I can't do it for someone else.
To let go is not to cut myself off,
it's the realization that I can't control another.
To let go is not to enable,
but to allow learning from natural consequences.
To let go is to admit powerlessness,
which means the outcome is not in my hands.
To let go is not to try to change or blame another,
I can only change myself.
To let go is not to care for,
but to care about.
To let go is not to fix,
but to be supportive.
To let go is not to judge,
but to allow another to be a human being.
To let go is not to be in the middle, arranging all the outcomes,
but to allow others to affect their own outcomes.
To let go is not to be protective; it is to permit another to face reality.
To let go is not to deny, but to accept.
To let go is not to nag, scold or argue, but to search out my own shortcomings and to correct them.
To let go is not to adjust everything to my desires, but to take each day as it comes.
To let go is not to criticize and regulate anyone, but to try to become what I dream I can be.
To let go is not to regret the past, but to grow and live for the future.
To let go is to fear less and love more![5]

CHAPTER 1

LETTING GO OF GRIEF

"She's not dead!" I shouted. "She's not! She's not!" I pounded my fist on my car's steering wheel in the mall parking lot.

Christmas shopping only a week after my mother's funeral devastated me. Making my way through a department store, I inhaled the aroma of fresh popcorn — the same aroma that filled the hallway to my mother's hospital room when the nurses brought the patients' nightly snack.

I hurried to the card section to find a Christmas card for my stepfather, but all I saw were row after row of "Mother" cards. I panicked, thinking, *I have to get out of here.* Exiting this particular store, however, meant going through the Toy Department stacked with boxes of Scrabble™ — the game my mother and I often played long past midnight, making up words so ridiculous they brought tears to our eyes.

Back in the car, I turned on the ignition, only to hear a voice from a Christian radio station say, "Perhaps it doesn't feel like Christmas to you. Maybe this is your first Christmas after the loss of a loved one."

That's when I pounded the steering wheel, insisting, "She's not dead! She's not!"

*****

The death of a loved one is a heart-wrenching experience. Even when you know they're Christians and you'll see them again, it isn't the same as seeing them face-to-face and talking with them. Faith doesn't always take away the pain and the aching loneliness.

Because my mother was sick for eighteen months before she died, I thought I was prepared. But eleven years later, I still could not cope with the reality that she was gone.

Day after day I looked at her picture and cried. I talked about her to whoever would listen, and I cried. Whenever someone mentioned her name, I cried. I often cried myself to sleep at night thinking about her, and awoke the next morning finding my pillow damp with tears. Singing her favorite song at church — or any song about heaven — caused pain.

She was on my mind constantly. The grief was so intense, it interfered with my everyday life. Friends were concerned, but I felt helpless to cope with it.

How Others Deal with Grief

During these years, friends of mine also experienced grief and I found that they each dealt with it in their own way. One older woman told me, "I went to New York, buried my mother, and that was it. I never gave her another thought. We never got along anyway."

In contrast, my friend Carol, a young pastor's wife who lost her thirteen-year-old son in a car/bicycle accident, wrote me several years after his death:

> "When the wound is emotional … we want instant restoration. I know that after we lost Brian, I almost immediately looked up the different stages of grief and information on how best to cope. I knew there was a process that had to be gone through, and I wanted to do it right the first time to make it as quick as possible. If there was a way to hurt fast and get it over with, I wanted to do it."

The FREEDOM of *Letting Go*

DON'T FEEL GUILTY FOR GRIEVING

I felt guilty for grieving because I was a Christian. After all, didn't the Bible say that we shouldn't sorrow as those who have no hope (1 Thessalonians 4:13)? However, as Mark Metcalfe writes, "Knowing Jesus does not mean He has taken away our grief or our loss."[1]

Doug Manning seemed to describe my feelings best in his book, *Don't Take My Grief Away:*

> "Right now your chest hurts ... The numbness has worn off and real pain has replaced it. You wonder if you will ever be well again ... [You find that] loneliness comes in only one size — Extra Large."[2]

He assures us that:

> "Grieving is as natural as crying when you are hurt, sleeping when you are tired or sneezing when your nose itches. It is nature's way of healing a broken heart."[3]

Manning shares the story of a couple that lost their eighteen-month-old daughter suddenly with croup. The mother cried hysterically. Friends said, "There, there, now get ahold of yourself. You can't carry on like this. Come on now — stop crying."

The mother looked at them with fire in her eyes and said, "Don't take my grief from me. I deserve it. I am going to have it."

"Don't let anyone take your grief from you," Manning says. "You deserve it, and you must have it. If you had broken a leg, no one would criticize you for using crutches until it was healed. If you had major surgery, no one would pressure you to run in a marathon the next week. Grief is a major wound. It does not heal overnight. You must have the time and the crutches until you heal."[4]

Don't Delay Your Grieving

A friend suggested that part of my problem could be because I didn't grieve at the time my mother died. This was probably true because I thought I had done much of my grieving during the eighteen months of her illness. Also, my grieving process was delayed because I was so busy.

At the time of my mother's death, I owned and operated a secretarial and income tax service. When I returned from her funeral in another state, it was mid-December. Because I had been with her since November 10, I had not addressed my Christmas cards or done any shopping. Returning to my office after the holidays, I was swamped with end-of-semester term papers and theses. When that part of my work slowed down, the tax business began and, after April 15, came another rush of college typing. So I didn't purposely delay the grieving process; I was just simply too busy to think about it.

Then, in June, my husband and I went back to clean out some of my mother's things. Walking into her house and seeing the empty recliner by the window hit me hard, and when I returned home, I went into an eighteen-month depression. At one time, I had thirty-nine jobs waiting to be completed for customers. As each person called, I would tell him or her that their work would be ready the next day, then I'd somehow find the strength to finish that one job.

During this time of depression, I tried to read the Bible and pray, but it seemed no one was listening. One day as I washed the dishes, tears ran down my cheeks. In desperation, I shook my fist at the heavens and yelled, "Is anyone up there? Is anybody listening?" Immediately, from the television set in the living room came these words: "The audio portion of this program is temporarily disrupted. Please stand by." The words couldn't have come at a better time. God was still listening; He wasn't giving up on me. I was to stand by and wait for the morning when, as His Word promises, joy would return: "Weeping may remain for a night, but rejoicing comes in the morning." (Psalm 30:5)

Find a Scripture Verse and Make It Yours

One other verse that helped me during this time was 2 Corinthians 1:3: "Who comforts us ... that we can comfort." I knew when this period of mourning was over, God would use me to help others.

John Henry Jowett writes concerning this verse:

> "And how does the Lord comfort us? He has a thousand different ways, and no one can ever tell by what way the comfort will come to his soul. Sometimes it comes by the door of memory, and sometimes by the door of hope ... other times through the ministry of human speech and kindness. But always, I think, it brings us the sense of a Presence, as though we had a great Friend in the room, and the troubled heart gains quietness and peace."[5]

Don't Let Others Tell You How — or How Long — to Grieve

I found that everyone had his or her own idea on how I should grieve and for how long.

"There will be those who will 'know' exactly how you should feel or act," Manning says ... "If you grieve too long, you are weak. If you don't grieve long enough, you did not love."[6]

He quotes a newspaper survey that asked people how long it took to mourn the loss of a loved one. Answers varied from forty-eight hours to two weeks, while clinical tests showed it takes from eighteen months to two years. The only ones who knew were those who had, themselves, experienced grief.

A friend on the Internet wrote me about losing her adopted five-year-old daughter. "People kept telling me to let go," she told me, "but I wasn't ready." She shared her feelings in a poem she wrote a year later: [7]

Time to Let Go

The other day a friend told me it was time to let go of Sarah, but let go of what?
In the last year since her death, I have:
Let go of the hand that I held while crossing many streets, in an effort to protect her from harm.
Let go of her body, which I lovingly bathed and dressed, hugged and held.
Let go of her mind, which I nurtured with books and stories and answers to endless questions.
Let go of her possessions; her raggedy blanket that was her constant companion; her stuffed animals, each with a name; her bike with its memories of long rides down by the river.
What are left are the memories — of her sweet smile, her giggle, her sparkling eyes and her love.
Please don't ask me to let go of them. They are all I have left of Sarah and I will treasure them forever.

"I hate the word 'closure,'" my sister told me shortly after she and her husband found their twenty-year-old grandson hanging in his bedroom at their house. "I don't want to put a closure on Andy's life. I'm not ready to let go of him yet."

Only you know when it's time to let go!

THE STAGES OF GRIEF

A speaker on a Christian radio talk show one day stated that the stages of grieving are similar to the stages of dying written about by Elizabeth Kubler-Ross. One of the stages of grieving mentioned by the radio was anger — not at God, but at the person who had died.

My first reaction upon hearing this was to vehemently disagree! I believed my anger (which I tried to suppress — being a Christian!) was directed toward God for not healing my mother. But that day, I realized I was angry at her! Angry because she didn't go to the doctor when she knew what was wrong. (It was the same disease that took my father, and she recognized the symptoms.) Angry because we could have enjoyed her longer. In fact, I was downright mad! I think that day began the start of my healing — the day I realized *it was okay to be angry.*

"I thought, as a Christian I had skipped over the grief step of anger," writes Ann Womack Lundberg, seven months after her husband's death. "I didn't want to be angry at God because I knew He wanted what was best for us, even if it meant taking a loved one home to be with Him. But I was angry. I was angry because my children's father would not be around to give them the wise counsel and love they needed from him. I was angry because our little granddaughters would not grow up to know the wonderful man their 'Papa Jim' was ... I was angry because a long-awaited time had been taken from us, when, with the children on their own, we could have more time together, slow down a little and enjoy a new phase in our life."[8]

Begin to Look Ahead

Eventually, the time will come when instead of spending your days looking in your rearview mirror, you will again begin to look forward to your tomorrows. Leona Choy wrote these words after she lost her husband:

> "God has a joyful, continuing assignment for her [the Christian widow] — but only after she walks slowly and deliberately over the natural bridge of the healthy grieving process which the Lord has provided. She should not be tempted to swing quickly like Tarzan across the chasm from loss to adjustment without that transition time. It is not done in an instant. Working through emotions and changes that come with human loss is often painstaking."[9]

The Beginning of Letting Go

Many things happened in the eleven years after my mother died that I wanted to share with her: books I wrote and sold, writing workshops I held across the country, our daughter's marriage to a very special son-in-law, our two beautiful granddaughters, and my husband's heart attack and forced retirement at forty-eight.

I wanted to ask her advice on family problems; invite her to go on trips with us; share news of friends with her. Many times I picked up the phone to call her, then hung up — remembering. It was almost like she was on a long vacation and would soon return. I just couldn't accept the finality of it.

One weekend, our family went to a motel in Tucson. I woke up at six o'clock Saturday morning and walked next door to the restaurant to get a cup of tea. Standing at the register, I was stunned to see a lady ahead of me who looked exactly like my mother — from the bun in her hair, to the flowered housedress with a tie-belt, to the old-fashioned pumps. She paid her bill and left, and I hurriedly tossed a dollar at the cashier and bolted out the door. Once outside I looked around everywhere, but the woman was gone.

Walking back to our motel room, I almost shouted into the semi-darkness, "God, will this hurt ever go away?"

I sensed a voice saying to me, "I've wanted to take it away, but you wouldn't give it to Me."

"Then take it," I cried. "I can't deal with it anymore."

THE NIGHT I SAID GOOD-BYE

My mother died on December 7, 1982. In 1993, after teaching at two writing workshops in Michigan, I rented a cottage for a week at our church campground. "I need to say good-bye to Mother," I told my sister, "and Indian Lake is the place I can do it."

Our family had attended our denominational ten-day camp meeting near Kalamazoo every year since I was eleven years old. After I left Michigan at the age of twenty, my mother — and later my stepfather — continued to go for another thirty-three years, and eventually bought a cabin there. When I thought of Mom, I thought of Indian Lake and vice versa.

I took six writing projects with me to the lake on Monday, and by Saturday I had finished all but one. During that week, several storms hit the area. One night, the wind blew tree limbs against the front window of the house where I was staying. Thunder clapped and lightning lit up the lakefront yard. Normally I loved storms, but now I was frightened. It was different being alone in a strange house.

On Saturday afternoon, while relaxing with a crossword puzzle, the radio station announced more storms that evening with "rain and damaging winds."

That did it. I was leaving! I headed to the pay phone to call the friends who were to pick me up on Monday. They weren't home. I called my brother. He wasn't home.

Back at the cottage, I sang the old song, "Master, the Tempest Is Raging." Then I dug through my suitcase (I had packed everything earlier to leave), and took out my Bible. To ease my fears, I read the story of the disciples in the boat and Christ's command, "Peace, be still." (Mark 4:39 KJV) I went through an old hymnal and sang comforting songs. And I prayed.

I prayed for my safety. I prayed for my family in Arizona. I prayed for those who had attended the recent writing workshops. Then I closed my prayer with my usual, "Lord, You know I want Your will."

By this time I could hear the storm all around me. Lightning flashed through the undraped windows, and the wind blew the shingles on the roof. Thunder roared so loud I held my ears. But, in the midst of this, I heard a quiet voice asking, "Did you want My will eleven years ago when I took your mother?"

The question startled me and I began to argue, "Lord, if only she had gone to the doctor sooner. She knew what was wrong. It was the same thing Dad died of. Her death was so senseless. She didn't have to die."

As an afterthought, I added, "And Lord, You *could* have healed her. She was a good woman. Even though she didn't make much from babysitting and ironing, she always paid her tithe and gave to the church building fund. She spent her whole life giving to others. So, Lord, *why* didn't You heal her?"

Again came that soft voice, "Because it was time."

Suddenly the words of a song my nephew wrote came to me:

I used to pray with answers already in my mind,
And wondered why His leading always seemed so hard to find;
But now I'm more dependent on His will instead of mine,
I'm learning how to live in God's own time.[10]

All at once, the truth became clear to me. How often in the past had God proved to me that His timing is always perfect.

"Okay, Lord," I yielded. "I give her to You. She's Yours."

The tears came again, but this time they weren't tears of loneliness and pain. They were tears of surrender, tears of relinquishment, tears of peace. The storm was still raging outside, but the storm in my heart was finally gone.

The Ship

I am standing upon the seashore. A ship at my side spreads her white sails to the morning breeze and starts for the blue ocean … I stand and watch her until at length she hangs like a speck of white cloud come down to mingle with each other. Then someone at my side says, "There! She's gone!"

Gone where? Gone from my sight … that is all. She is just as large in mast and hull and spar as she was when she left my side … Her diminished size is in me, not in her. And just at the moment when someone at my side says, "There! She's gone!" there are eyes on the other shore watching her coming and other voices ready to take up the glad shout, "Here she comes!"

And that is dying.[11]

CHAPTER 2

Letting Go of Failures — Your Own and Other People's

My husband, Gary, wasn't brought up in church, but when he was sixteen years old, a friend's grandmother paid taxi fare each Sunday for her grandson and three of his friends to get to church. One of these friends was Gary, and during a series of special meetings, he became a Christian.

The night Gary accepted Christ, the speaker laid his hands on his head and said, "This young man is called to the ministry." Not having any religious background on how to know God's will, Gary accepted this as a call, and after graduating from high school, he enrolled in Bible college.

After two years, he wanted to change his major to education, but he felt guilty going against what he thought was God's will for his life, so he continued with his ministerial studies. Upon graduation, he attended seminary for two years, and later accepted a small church. ("Small" is an understatement, as they paid him ten dollars a week, and then offered the custodian fifteen dollars. You could also add the word "challenging." A nearby minister said being the pastor of that particular church was like coming in as a relief pitcher in the ninth inning of a ballgame with bases loaded and Babe Ruth coming up to bat.)

After one very stressful year, he resigned, due to family health problems. We then moved to my hometown where we joined my home

The FREEDOM of *Letting Go*

church. Gary later shared with our pastor that he now felt he wasn't called to preach after all. The pastor responded by saying perhaps God allowed him to fail at his church to show him he wasn't called.

Because of the pastor's comment, Gary felt like a failure for resigning the church after only one year — the church he felt the Lord had called him to.

But had he failed? During this single year of his pastorate, our two-year-old daughter — who wasn't expected to live long enough to attend kindergarten — was healed, a mother of seven accepted the Lord and she and her family began attending church, and the Sunday school superintendent's sister and husband were reunited through our counseling. Also, the hearts of our agnostic neighbors were softened through our daughter's healing and they allowed their son to participate in a talent night at the church.

When I am left with shattered plans, He has a better set of plans.
(Pamela Reeve)

We can feel like a failure in many ways. Our employers, our parents, and even our church leaders sometimes hold up such high standards, we feel like failures if we can't reach them. John Snider says that, "The risk of failing is so great that we'd prefer not to take any chances." He adds,

> "Many Christians are afraid of failure … Maybe it stems from the mistaken belief that failure indicates one is 'out of step' with God. Often we look up to a spiritual model such as a television evangelist, our pastor or a leader in our church and assume that his or her 'special' relationship with God prevents him from failing at anything."[1]

Mothers and wives can feel like failures as they compare themselves to others in their neighborhood or church, not seeing the different circumstances beneath the surface of each life. Snider tells of one woman with two children under three who felt that in order to be a good housewife, she must not only care for the kids, but keep the house immaculate at all times. Discouragement crowded out her joy because she failed to meet her impossible standards. "She needs to accept her humanness," Snider says, "and lower her unnecessarily high expectations."[2]

I will never forget one speaker's comment on Christians being human. He said, "Lady, if you've just finished hanging your white sheets on the line, and the neighbor dog comes over, pulls them down and drags them through the dirt, and you say, 'Praise the Lord, my neighbor's dog just pulled my sheets down, and is dragging them through the mud,' then lady, go up to heaven with the saints and let us mortals be!"

Work

Work-connected failure can take many forms. For Christians, it may simply be a lack of knowing what God has called them to do. In Chapter 10, I share my experience when I felt called to be a medical missionary, but left nurse's training after only three months. I felt like a failure because my church had backed me, and I had shared my call at a number of church events. It took several years before the Lord showed me that my mission field was in spreading the gospel through the printed page.

You can feel like a failure when you don't get the dream job you apply for. *I have the education and skills the job called for, so why did it go to someone else?,* you wonder. The same feeling of failure can crop up when you don't get a promotion you hope for, and the position goes to someone less qualified.

You can also experience a great sense of failure when you are laid off or fired from a job. Many people who lose jobs, however, in looking back count it a blessing. This dark time often transforms into the chance to reach for a dream they have long held, such as owning their own business. Or perhaps the loss leads to discovering a talent they didn't know they possessed.

From every failure I have learned two equally valuable lessons: There was at least one reason why I failed, and I can rebound from that failure. (Harvey Mackay)

My friend Pam was an assistant manager at a fast food restaurant. The manager was unbearable to work for, and Pam got fired for the first time in her life. "I was hurt and angry," she said, "and yet it was like a big burden was lifted from me." Pam goes on to say,

"I needed chiropractic treatment and couldn't afford it with no job, so I found a new chiropractor who was looking for help, and I offered to work out a trade. I would work on his busy days for getting the adjustments I needed. After the end of the first week, he unexpectedly gave me a paycheck. I now had a job again, with less hours and stress and better pay. After a few years he paid for me to go to school where I discovered I had a gift with massage. Eventually, I started my own business."

Another friend shares that she'll always remember when her husband was laid off. "So many people expressed their sadness and concern," she said. "But one guy grabbed our hands and his eyes twinkled. His voice held an unmistakable excitement as he said,

'This is so exciting. I can't wait to see what God has ahead for you!' It totally changed our outlook," she admits.

Gordon Chilvers says, "Being human, we all fail at something at some time. No one succeeds all the time. The most successful people in the world have failed at least once."[3] This is graphically illustrated by the following examples:

- Walt Disney formed his first animation company in Kansas City in 1921. He made a deal with a distribution company in New York, in which he would ship them his cartoons and get paid six months down the road. He began to experiment with new storytelling techniques, his costs went up and then the distributor went bankrupt. He was forced to dissolve his company and at one point could not pay his rent and was surviving by eating dog food. When he tried to get MGM studios to distribute Mickey Mouse in 1927, he was told that the idea would never work — a giant mouse on the screen would terrify women.
- Winston Churchill failed sixth grade. He was subsequently defeated in every election for public office until he became prime minister at the age of sixty-two.
- Henry Ford could not read or write, failed and went broke five times in business before he succeeded.
- Van Gogh sold only one painting during his life — to the sister of one of his friends, for four-hundred francs (approximately fifty dollars). This didn't stop him from completing more than eight-hundred paintings.
- Babe Ruth, who held the homerun record (until surpassed by Hank Aaron), also holds the record for 1,330 strikeouts.
- In the music field, Decca Records turned down a recording contract with The Beatles with the evaluation, "We don't like

their sound. Groups of guitars are on their way out." After Decca rejected the Beatles, Columbia records followed suit. And in 1954, Jimmy Denny, manager of the Grand Ole Opry, fired Elvis Presley after one performance. He told Presley, "You ain't goin' nowhere, son. You ought to go back to drivin' a truck."[4]

Many of life's failures are people who did not realize how close they were to success when they gave up. (Thomas Alva Edison)

Parents

Joe was born into a family of Sicilian immigrants. For more than three-hundred years his ancestors had made their living as fishermen; however, the smell of raw fish and the motion of a rocking boat made Joe sick. His family considered him a failure, especially his dad who referred to him as "good for nothing."

Joe felt that his attempts at other types of work were an admission of failure. One thing he could do, however, was play baseball. Giving up an occupation where he could not succeed, Joe DiMaggio moved to another area and became one of the greatest players in baseball history.[5]

Sometimes our parents unintentionally make us feel like failures. I remember overwhelming our daughter with advice upon the birth of her firstborn. One day, I complimented her for something and she responded, "You mean I'm doing *something* right?"

John Snider said that, unintentionally, his parents gave him the message that he "couldn't do anything right."

"[They created in me] a *fear* of failure. All they wanted to do, they said, was keep me from making mistakes. So when I'd sit down with Dad to build model airplanes and would arrive at a difficult

step, he'd glue the joint for me so I wouldn't 'mess it up.' And Mom always seemed to discourage me from trying anything new …
"Over a long period of time, this constant overprotection from my parents worked its way into my system. I began to feel that failing at something, or even making a mistake, would cause irreversible damage to my character. Even today, I hesitate before starting a new project, worrying that maybe I'll do a poor or inadequate job."[6]

Teachers

Often an innocent remark by a teacher can haunt a child's mind forever. A friend shared with me that when she turned in a paper in elementary school, the teacher accused her of copying it out of a book. "I know you can't write that well," she told the student. It wasn't until my friend was close to retirement age that she picked up her writing dream again.

Another example is Albert Einstein, who did not speak until he was four years old and did not read until he was seven. His parents thought he was "sub-normal," and one of his teachers described him as "mentally slow, unsociable, and adrift forever in foolish dreams." He was expelled from school and was refused admittance to the Zurich Polytechnic School. He did eventually learn to speak and read, even to do a little math.[7]

When my brother and I were in the fifth and sixth grade, we were in the same room. The teacher would often compare our work, saying to me, "Why can't you draw like your brother?" and to him, "Why can't you write like your sister?" (Unfortunately for me, I still can't draw but he writes songs and beautiful poetry.)

These casual comments don't have to lead to a feeling of failure, however. This same teacher would often tear up my work, saying,

"You can do better than that." Or she would return it with myriad red marks. This challenged me. I determined to write something and have it returned with *no* red marks — and I finally succeeded. Rather than let her words discourage me, they motivated me to be a better writer.

Children

One writer friend wrote a poem, which she shared with her young daughter. When she finished, her daughter said, "You call *that* a poem?!"

Another friend shared that she attended her high school daughter's choir concert.

"It was incredible," she said. "My shy little girl had turned into a true performer, singing and dancing to some upbeat music. Her beauty shone in everything she did. I shed tears, I was so proud, and couldn't wait to hug her and congratulate her when the concert ended — unaware that teens are often embarrassed when their parents carry on about all they do. I rushed to the front of the auditorium, but she ignored me, turning away from my breathless advance toward her. I wondered, 'Did I teach her to not honor her parent?' I felt such failure, it overshadowed being blessed that God gave me such a beautiful, talented daughter."

Ourselves

Sometimes we are harder on ourselves than we are on others, or than others are on us. If we have actually failed, then we need to ask for God's help, forgive ourselves, and move on.

Our pastor defines a failure as one who thinks about doing things, but never does them. He said he's buried a lot of people with the music still in them; their song has never been sung. He adds that the failure itself is not the problem; it's our attitude toward it. Our failures can be springboards or stumbling blocks. Thus, it's not what happens to us, it's what happens in us.

We need to let go of our failures. A mother returned home from a neighbor's house one day. As she walked into the house, she saw five of her youngest children huddled together, concentrating on something. As she drew near them trying to discover the object of their attention, she couldn't believe her eyes. Smack dab in the middle of the circle were several baby skunks. She screamed at the top of her voice, "Children, run!" *Each kid grabbed a skunk and ran!*

Don't run into the future dragging your past failures with you. A line from a '50s song says, "Let the past just fade away; why be lost in yesterday?" Don't let your failures ruin the rest of your life.

A speaker at a camp meeting shared that, when he was a small boy, his dad picked up a piece of wood and asked if his son would like a baseball bat. Sure, the boy replied, what boy wouldn't? Every day, the son ran into the woodshop to see if the bat was finished, but every day the slab of wood was still in the corner, covered with shavings. One day — impatient with his father's slowness — he decided to make his own bat, so he climbed up on a sawhorse, took his dad's hatchet down from the shelf and began whittling away. In the process, he ruined the piece of wood. In tears, he took it back to his dad, who shaved a piece of wood off here, another there, and eventually handed the boy a beautiful bat.

"Some of us have knifed our life to pieces," the speaker said. "We've used a hatchet on it, axed it up, and made a mess of it. But when we turn it over to God, He can give us back a beautiful life."

The FREEDOM of *Letting Go*

After a day in the streams of the Scottish highlands, some fishing companions gathered at a small inn for tea. As one of them was describing the day's exploits, the waitress set down a cup of tea. A hand flew out and hit the teacup, knocking its contents against the whitewashed wall. An ugly brown stain appeared, marring the beautiful finish.

One of the other guests rose to his feet and said, "Never mind." Taking a crayon from his pocket, he began to sketch around the stain. There emerged a magnificent stag with antlers spread. The man was Sir Edwin Landseer, England's foremost painter of animals.

If an artist can do that with an ugly stain, I've often thought, what cannot God do with my mistakes if only I'll turn them over to Him. [8]

Letting Go of Other People's Failures

Often when we can't forgive ourselves and let go of our failures, we also find it difficult to forgive others for their failures. It's so easy to remind family members of mistakes and wrong decisions they made in the past — especially if we feel responsible for those mistakes. We say, "If only I hadn't said such-and-such to them, our children wouldn't have rebelled."

"If only I had been a better wife, my husband wouldn't have left."

"If we hadn't charged so many things when our children were young, they wouldn't have so many debts now."

How to Deal with Failure

John Snider gives the following suggestions on dealing with failure:

1. Ask yourself: Have I truly failed, or am I simply not meeting unrealistic expectations?

2. [If you decide you truly failed], try to determine why ... consider both the obvious and below-the-surface reasons.

3. Allow yourself to fully experience any feelings of anger, bitterness, remorse, etc., over your failure. If you don't get them off your chest, they'll eat away at you, making it harder still to learn from your failure.

4. Ask: Which doors, if any, has this failure closed for me? Which has it opened? What strengths does this failure point me toward? (Your conclusion here could be simply, "Work harder." But it could also signal a bigger change ahead for you.)

5. Consider God's perspective. How is God using this failure to direct your life?

6. Accept yourself as you are before you try to be anything different. Failure in a task doesn't mean you're a failure as a person. Relax. Give yourself a break.

Snider had been laid off his job, but he ended up getting another job better than the previous one. "Who knows where I'd be now if I hadn't failed earlier," he says.[9]

FAILURE ISN'T THE END
Wightman Weese, in his book, *Back in Touch,* says,

> "Right now, if you are depressed about failure, think about the valuable person you are and how much more useful you will become when you let God help you make your way back.

The FREEDOM of *Letting Go*

"When you have recovered, you will ... recognize other hurting people ... in ways that you never did before ... In the days ahead you may be the person God uses to help them make a comeback too. Then you may even be able to thank God for what you have gone through, and for teaching you lessons you couldn't have learned any other way."[10]

A past failure does not mean at all that you have established a pattern. A little seven-year-old boy fell out of an apple tree and broke his wrist. As he looked at the ugly hump, he said to the doctor, "My wrist will never be strong, will it? And if I break my arm again, won't it always break in the same place?"

The doctor said, "No, Joe. When we have properly set the bone and put it in a cast till it has healed, then this will be the strongest place in your arm. And if you should ever have another break, depend on it, it won't be here."[11]

- *Lost job, 1832*
- *Defeated for legislature, 1832*
- *Failed in business, 1833*
- *Elected to legislature, 1834*
- *Sweetheart (Ann Rutledge) died, 1835*
- *Had nervous breakdown, 1836*
- *Defeated for Speaker, 1838*
- *Defeated for nomination for Congress, 1843*
- *Elected to Congress, 1846*
- *Lost re-nomination, 1848*
- *Rejected for land officer, 1849*
- *Defeated for Senate, 1854*
- *Defeated for nomination for vice-president, 1856*

- *Again defeated for Senate, 1858*
- *Elected president, 1860*

Who is the above referring to? Abraham Lincoln![12]

At the age of twenty, I began a dream job as secretary to the book editor at our church publishing house. I arrived in the middle of a two-year textbook project, written by more than two-dozen theologians across the United States. I had to keep track of each chapter as it arrived, retype the edited pages, and check permissions. Finally it was done, and my employer's wife came in for two weeks and prepared the index.

Cleaning out the cabinets after the book was sent to production, I found a section of the manuscript from the center of the book that had been missed in all the back-and-forth process. This threw off all the index pages from that section on, and I groaned, knowing it would cause repeated work by the wife.

I walked to church that night, failure hanging over my head like a black cloud. *How could I do such a stupid thing? I'm such an idiot. I'll probably be fired tomorrow, then I'll have to go back home in disgrace and everyone will know I'm a complete failure.*

Later in the service, the pastor gave a prayer, part of which I have never forgotten. "Lord," he prayed, "help us to wait upon You, help us to mount up with wings as eagles, and Lord, give us pedestrian grace so we can walk and not faint." (Note: I wasn't fired and stayed at the job for two more years. And the phrase "pedestrian grace" led to a devotional book on Isaiah 40:31.)

Whether you've been running in your life through major crises or walking through mundane chores, whether you are an employer or an employee, a teacher or a student, a parent or a child, you will fail in your task at least once and probably more. But that isn't the end of your life. God can take that mistake, that failure, and turn it into a beautiful experience.

In the Louvre in Paris, there is a painting called *Faust*. It is a painting of a chess game. On one side of the chessboard is Mephistopheles, a manifestation of the devil. Opposite him is Faust, with whom he has made an infamous pact. Mephistopheles is pointing at the board with a heinous look of triumph. You can almost hear him say, "Checkmate!" Faust is cowering on the other side.

A Grand Master chess player was looking at this painting one day, feeling the despair of it, when suddenly he jumped at the painting and shouted, "Wait a minute! Wait a minute! Faust still has one move!"[13]

And that's the message for you today. No matter how much you feel you have failed, don't give up. In God's mercy and grace, you still have one more move — and that's upward. The Lord will turn your failure into triumph!

Failure doesn't mean you are a failure ...
It does mean you haven't succeeded yet.

Failure doesn't mean you have accomplished nothing ...
It does mean you have learned something.

Failure doesn't mean you have been a fool ...
It does mean you had a lot of faith.

Failure doesn't mean you've been disgraced ...
It does mean you were willing to try.

Failure doesn't mean you don't have it ...
It does mean you have to do something in a different way.

Donna Clark Goodrich

Failure doesn't mean you are inferior ...
It does mean you are not perfect.

Failure doesn't mean you've wasted your life ...
It does mean you have a reason to start afresh.

Failure doesn't mean you should give up ...
It does mean you must try harder.

Failure doesn't mean you'll never make it ...
It does mean it will take a little longer.

Failure doesn't mean God has abandoned you ...
It does mean God has a better idea.[14]

He Covered My Scars with Love

My body held bruises from the lessons that life had me learn
All the scars and the secrets in the places that sin had me burned
When I thought I was living, I thought I was dying
In a way I had not seen before
But when I met Jesus, He covered my scars,
And they'll never be seen anymore.

Now my scars, they're all gone, but the memory is still in my mind
Of the days that I wasted when help was right there all the time
With my life sinking lower and my scars growing wider
It seemed all I could see was the end
But His love reached down deeper and He covered my scars
And they'll never be seen again.

The FREEDOM of *Letting Go*

For He covered my scars with love
And He washed them away with His blood
He took all the places
Where my life was wasted
And He covered my scars with His love.[15]

CHAPTER 3

LETTING GO OF YOUR SUCCESSES

WHAT IS SUCCESS?

How do you know if you're successful? If you're a writer, do you measure success in terms of how many articles you've sold, or if your book has won an award or reached the Top 10 in sales? If you're a teacher, does your success depend on how far your students go after they leave your classroom? If you're a mother, do you judge your success by your children's spiritual maturity?

My mother used to quote the saying, "God has no grandchildren; only children," signifying that because parents are Christians doesn't mean their children will automatically end up serving the Lord.

I heard a story about an evangelist who held a series of special meetings at a church. Before the Sunday morning service, he spoke to a Sunday school class of middle-age couples. The teacher introduced him with these words: "We know his walk with God has been successful by the fact that all of his children have accepted the Lord and are in full-time Christian ministry."

One mother, who had spent many sleepless nights praying for her son's salvation, looked around the room and saw a number of godly parents whose children had not accepted the Lord. Did this mean that their walk with God was not successful?

The FREEDOM of *Letting Go*

Letting Go of Our Successes

Our preacher said one Sunday that we should "rehearse our successes." In other words, we should recall them from time to time — not in pride, but "because God gave us the successes." And because God gave them to us, we need to let go of them and move forward.

Hannah Whitall Smith says, in *The Christian's Secret of a Happy Life,*

> "Never indulge at the close of an action, in any self-reflective acts of any kind, whether of self-congratulation or of self-despair. Forget the things that are behind the moment they're past, leaving them with God … When the temptation comes, as it always does, to indulge in these reflections, either of one sort or the other, I turn from them at once and positively refuse to think about my work at all, leaving it with the Lord to overrule the mistakes, and to bless it as He chooses."[1]

Someone once said that there is no limit to how much can be done in the world if no one cares who gets the credit. It's odd that when something goes wrong, no one wants to take the blame, but when a project succeeds, suddenly everyone wants the accolades.

A frog wanted to go south for the winter, but he felt it would take much too long to hop. So, being a rather clever fellow, he persuaded two large geese to hold a stick between their bills for him to grasp firmly with his teeth, thus hitching a free ride to a warmer climate. The trip went well until a farmer happened to see the strange trio flying overhead.

"Do you see what I see?" said the farmer to his son. "I wonder who in the world was clever enough to convince the geese to take him south?"

High overhead, the frog heard the conversation and his chest puffed out with pride. Unable to contain himself, he shouted, "I did," upon which he let go of the stick and plunged to Earth.

When you've completed a successful endeavor and someone asks, "Who did it," you don't have to shout out, "I did!" Your downfall might just follow sooner than you think.

Successful Failures

Bill Bright, in his booklet, *Jesus and the Intellectual,* tells the following story:

"In 1923, an important meeting was held at the Edgewater Beach Hotel in Chicago. Attending this meeting were nine of the world's most successful financiers: Charles Schwab, president of the largest independent steel company; Samuel Insull, president of the largest utility company; Howard Hopson, president of the largest gas company; Arthur Cotton, the greatest wheat speculator; Richard Whitney, president of the New York stock exchange; Albert Fall, a member of the President's cabinet; Leon Fraser, president of the Bank of International Settlements; Jesse Livermore, the greatest 'bear' on Wall Street; and Ivar Krueger, head of the greatest monopoly.

"Twenty-five years later, Charles Schwab had died in bankruptcy, having lived on borrowed money for five years before his death; Samuel Insull had died a fugitive from justice, and penniless in a foreign land; Howard Hopson was insane; Arthur Cotton had died abroad, insolvent; Richard Whitney had spent time in Sing Sing; Albert Fall had been pardoned so that he could die at home; Jesse Livermore, Ivar Krueger and Leon Fraser had all died by suicide."

In man's eyes, the men listed appeared successful; however, as Bright concluded, "All of these men had learned well the art of making a living, but none of them had learned how to live."[2]

Remember not the former things that you have done, but remember the former things that God has done. (Ira Brown)

Fear of Success

It sounds strange, but some people are actually afraid to succeed. We work hard and accomplish a worthwhile endeavor for which we receive praise, and suddenly we're afraid that people will expect us to do that well every time. We ask ourselves, "What if I can't reach such a high standard again? If I do well, they will expect more from me. They'll think I can always do it." So what do we do? We quit!

Bob Phillips, in *42 Days to Feeling Great,* writes:

> "As strange as it seems, some people are fearful of achieving ... These individuals usually have low self-image; they cannot see themselves as successful ... Being a success would mean that their lifestyles would have to change. Being successful means they would have to face the fear of the unknown, the fear of rejection, and the burden and commitment to continue to succeed. Often this causes so much turmoil that they will disrupt their success. This gives them the freedom to return to the familiar territory of being average or even being failures."[3]

Dangers of Success

J. Carl Laney says that, "The danger that comes from being successful is that we begin to trust in ourselves — our own abilities, position of influence and resources, rather than God's."[4]

In 2 Chronicles we read, "But after Uzziah became powerful, his pride led to his downfall. He was unfaithful to the LORD his God" (26:16). As a result, God disciplined him and he lived out his days as a leper.

Talent is God-given, be humble. Fame is man-given, be thankful. Conceit is self-given, be careful. (John Madden)

Another danger of success is that you may incur the jealousy of those friends who see in you what they could have become, if only they had put forth the effort.

WHY BE SUCCESSFUL?

Why do people want to be successful? If it's to answer God's call or simply to reach a worthwhile goal, that's admirable. But if it's for the praise of men, that's the wrong reason. Pride may be the furthest thing from our mind and certainly not the reason that moves us to do something, but Satan can discourage us from becoming successful by telling us we're doing it for the wrong motive. One woman gave up playing the piano at church for that reason. She had known people who did things for their own glory and it turned her off. Satan used that to bully her, suggesting that she was playing merely to obtain the praise of people. He is shrewd, and he knows how to defeat us.

A songwriter, new to the business, heard that a well-known singer was going to record one of his songs. "I did the worst thing you can do in Nashville," he admitted. "I told everyone." Then the singer chose another song. The songwriter went home that night and wrote down all the reasons he wanted that singer to record his song. Looking at the list, he saw that not one of the reasons was acceptable in God's sight. So what did he do? He wrote a song about it.

> I spent my days searching
> for a high prize to gain
> but the sweetness of victory
> it was tasted in vain
> I did all the right things
> but the reasons were wrong
> I was lifting the singer
> Instead of the song[5]

THE SECRET TO SUCCESS

The secret to success can be found as we read God's Word. First, as shown in Joshua 1:7, we must *obey the law* so we may have success wherever we go. The complete verse says, "Be strong and very courageous. Be careful to obey all the law my servant Moses gave you; do not turn from it to the right or to the left, that you may be successful wherever you go."

Second, we must *be on God's side*. First Samuel 18:14 tells us that, "In everything he [David] did he had great success, because the LORD was with him." We cannot ask God for success in our undertaking if we're attempting to go against His will.

Third, we must *seek God's will*. "As long as he [Uzziah] sought the LORD, God gave him success." (2 Chronicles 26:5)

And fourth, we *shouldn't become discouraged*. "Then you will have success if you are careful to observe the decrees and laws that the LORD gave Moses for Israel. Be strong and courageous. Do not be afraid or discouraged." (1 Chronicles 22:13) Many writers never would have found success in the literary world if they had become discouraged and given up. For example, Margaret Mitchell's *Gone with the Wind* was turned down by more than twenty-five publishers. One claimed that, "The public is not interested in Civil War stories." And Jack London received six-hundred rejection slips before he sold his first story.

One thing to remember is that many authors of literary fame have received only worldly acclaim. Awards are great, as they signify men's approval, but they are not eternal. Trophies collect dust. Certificates of merit become yellowed with age. Dinners in our honor may be forgotten as soon as the attendees have left the banquet hall. These are the ones we are to let go of, as they are only temporary. God's rewards last for eternity.

The Rewards of Success

In the chapter on letting go of grief, I share that it took me eleven years to let go of my mother after her death. I wrote an article entitled, "The Night I Told Mother Goodbye," which appeared in *Decision* magazine. This was my first acceptance in this periodical and I was very thrilled.

More than the excitement of the sale, however, and even more than the check I received, was a letter I got from a gentleman whose wife had died nine years before. He shared his loneliness and the bitterness he had experienced against God during this difficult period. Then he closed his letter by saying, "But now I realize it was time. And thanks to your article, I can go on with my life."

In God's eyes, that is success!

CHAPTER 4

LETTING GO OF POSSESSIONS

Possessions, in and of themselves, are not wrong. However, as Rick and Bonnie Ryding point out in their article, "Enough Is Enough,"

"Goods and commitments ... require more money to maintain them, more space to house them and more time to tend them. It may be that we cease to own things, and they begin to own us ... When do we say 'Enough!'"[1]

We don't realize how important — or unimportant — our possessions have become until we don't have them. Cecil Murphey, author of the bestselling book, *Ninety Minutes in Heaven,* shares that when his family returned after nearly six years in Kenya, they owned nothing but their clothes (all badly out of style), a portable typewriter, and six crates of books. He enrolled in seminary, they rented an unfurnished apartment, and started life again with no possessions. A church gave them beds, someone in the student complex donated a sofa, and someone else donated a TV, ironing board, and a few other household items. "As we acquired each thing, we accepted them as special gifts and valued each item highly," he said. "We had nothing and anything looked wonderful."

Over the years, Cecil and his wife acquired more things, better-quality furniture, plenty of clothes, a computer, and (of course) more books. Then the unthinkable happened. In 2007, their house burned down and they lost all their possessions. For the second time, it meant beginning again with new clothes, furniture, a computer, a car — the obvious things. This time he also lost his library, which meant a great deal to him.

"My wife, Shirley, and I started over again," Cecil said. "And we found that beginning again is more than accumulating new possessions. It means a chance to leave behind old patterns of behavior ... To make a new start demands drastic changes. It involves uncertainty about the present as well as the future ... Not everyone can face that kind of challenge. It's safer and easier not to change. I wouldn't have started over again if I hadn't been forced to do so, yet I'm grateful I've been able to rethink my life."

Marjorie Holmes tells of a friend who lived in a beautiful home that she and her husband had worked so hard to acquire. It was finally furnished the way she wanted it. She was surrounded by Oriental rugs, formal French sofas, paintings, china, silver. Then she died — in the midst of her possessions. She was snatched away, while they remained.[2]

CREDIT CARD BUYING

Accumulating possessions often requires spending more than we take in, which can lead to the excessive use of credit cards. And this misuse of plastic not only causes tension in marriage, but it creates stress and upheaval in our personal lives. We work long hours, only to see our earnings eaten up in credit card payments and excessive interest.

Help us today, Lord, to sit on our credit cards and stand on Your promises. (author unknown)

The FREEDOM of *Letting Go*

We can give ourselves all kinds of reasons for our plastic spending, but the truth is, we're addicted to buying — the same as a person is addicted to taking drugs or drinking alcohol. This was my problem.

"Lord, You know I want to write more, but I just don't have the time," I cried one day. "You know how hard I work just to keep up with all the payments we have to make." (This clearly proved what author and speaker, Harold Ivan Smith, said at a writers' conference: "We won't reach our dreams because we're too wrapped up in plastic.")

That's when God reminded me that I wouldn't have to work so hard if I didn't charge so much. He was right. My addiction to plastic not only forced me to work long hours in my home business, but it also caused problems in our marriage.

Every time my husband thought we were getting caught up, another bill came in from a credit card he didn't know we had. It was so easy. The pre-approved letters came in the mail and all I had to do was sign my name. "This is the last one," I promised myself. "It's low-interest and I'll just use it to pay off a higher-interest bill, then I'll cut it up." But then I'd see something I wanted, something I "just couldn't wait for," and out came the new card.

Every spending decision is a spiritual decision.

It was easy for me to excuse myself by saying that our family didn't have much when I was young (my father had left when I was eleven, leaving my mother to raise three children alone), that I had to have something for my business or that I was helping our children. But the truth was, I was a slave to possessions.

One day a godly counselor pointed out to me that, because I

had been hurt by people earlier in my life, I felt safe buying things, as then I was in control. "Things" couldn't hurt me as people had.

That helped me understand "why" I bought so many things, but how to change became the challenge. Then our pastor said one Sunday, "Unmanageable finances are symptoms of an unmanageable life. We have misplaced our priorities and have put material things ahead of God. Things cannot fill the emptiness in our lives, only God can."

His words pierced my heart. I came home from church that morning and prayed that God would be Lord of *all* my life, especially the financial part. And since that day, with His help, I successfully began to break the plastic habit.

First, I cut up all my cards but one, and I left that card at home when I went shopping. Next, I waited twenty-four hours before buying something and discovered that, often by the next day, the desire had left. And I began paying cash, finding it much harder to hand over real money.

I also began sorting through things I already had, and in the next few years, I sold, gave away or threw away, literally, dozens of bags of "stuff."

Signs You Are Broke
- *You can't even pay attention.*
- *You stop getting offers from credit card companies trying to get you to transfer your other credit card balances to theirs.*
- *You forget whose picture is on a Lincoln penny.*
- *American Express calls and says: "Leave home without it!"*
- *Long distance companies don't call you to switch.*
- *You finally clean your house, hoping to find change.*
- *McDonald's supplies you with all your kitchen condiments.*
- *At communion, you go back for seconds.*[3]

The FREEDOM of *Letting Go*

Pack Rats

Often, people who have a "pack rat" mentality may also have a psychological problem. When we moved my elderly uncle out of a small travel trailer, it took me — with the help of my daughter and family — more than a week to clean out all his stuff: one-hundred eighty-five shirts, many with the price tags still on them; thirty-nine jackets; stacks of newspapers and plastic bags; broken statues he had picked up in alleys; numerous unopened packages of paper cups, plates, and napkins, and so on.

We moved him into an assisted living center, and later, when he went to an assisted living facility, we figured we could clean out his one room in an hour or so. Wrong! Somehow, he had managed to squeeze stuff into every inch of his closet — on the floor, the rods, and the shelves, and into four desk drawers and six dresser drawers, along with numerous boxes under the bed. Three sink drawers were filled to the top with sugar, salt and pepper packets, and napkins from restaurants, and a vegetable drawer in the refrigerator held butter packets from the dining room where he lived. (Later, we discovered he had also rented space in three storage facilities, but we never found out their contents, as he hadn't paid the monthly rent and the items were sold.)

I could partially understand his hoarding, as twice in his life he had lost everything he owned because of fires. This isn't the case with most of us, however.

What We Don't Use, We Store

Storage facility operators are capitalizing on a constant of modern culture: *Americans own a lot of stuff.*

According to the Self Storage Association (SSA), self-storage has been the fastest-growing sector of the U.S. commercial real estate market for the last thirty years, growing into a $220-billion industry.[4]

I read a story of an adult daughter who lived at home with her parents, but rented a storage space to keep all her extra stuff. Someone asked her when she had last retrieved something from the unit and she replied, "I haven't been over there in months." The friend then asked her how much she was paying each month to store her things. She said $33 a month, plus insurance. Annual total — $396 for rent, $132 for insurance, and $28 in state sales tax — all for storing things she never used.

When she realized the foolishness of her actions, she removed her things from the storage unit and had a garage sale — making enough to pay off a credit card debt, thus freeing her from two monthly payments.

How to Eliminate Clutter

If your house is cluttered with things you no longer need, here are some suggestions:

- Begin with one room, and select one drawer, one shelf, one cupboard or one closet.
- Remove everything, and then begin to sort.
- Make four piles: keep, toss, donate, and sell.
- If you have grown children, allow them to take what they want (better now than to have them fight over things after you're gone).
- Donate what you don't need or haven't used in a year, or hold a yard sale. If you can't bear to part with things, ask a friend to help you.

It helped me to make a chart listing what I wanted to tackle each week. It was fun crossing things off as I finished each one.

Compulsive Buying

Amy Bjork Harris says,

> "Many of us are compulsive buyers. Even as we trip over our latest acquisition, we head for the store to add to the collection. It's worth asking ourselves: how much is enough? Things demand attention: they must be dusted, stored, protected and insured. We pay for them with time as well as money ... Is the enjoyment you feel in acquiring worth the long-term price you pay?"[5]

A Christian magazine reported that a songbook had a misprint in one line of the hymn, *Guide Me, O Thou Great Jehovah*. Instead of "Land me safe on Canaan's shore," it read, "Land my safe on Canaan's shore."[6] Unfortunately, neither your safe nor any of your belongings will accompany you to the Promised Land.

Before you buy something, ask yourself the following questions:

1. Do I need it?
2. Will I use it?
3. Do I have something else that will work?
4. Have I gotten along without it so far?
5. Do I have room for it?
6. Will it take the place of something I can get rid of?
7. Do I have the money to buy it?
8. Can I get it cheaper somewhere else?
9. Can I ask for it as a gift?
10. Why do I want this? (honestly!)
11. Will it end up in a yard sale?
12. What will happen to it when I'm gone?

Donna Clark Goodrich

Don't be obsessed with getting more material things.
Be relaxed with what you have. (Hebrews 13:5 MSG)

Culture

Sometimes we buy things just because society says we need them to be successful. We have to have a certain job, we have to live in a certain neighborhood, drive a certain make of automobile, and live in a certain house. Then we've made it — or so we think. After a while, this job, this automobile, this house begin to take over all of our time and become our number one priority. We work long hours — for our family, we tell ourselves. We spend Saturdays and Sundays polishing the car, or remodeling the house that we thought was so perfect when we bought it. Our dream ends up becoming a nightmare.

A friend related to me about a lunch she had with a coworker. Having an administrative position in the company enabled this coworker to buy a high-priced automobile he had long wanted. All the time they were eating, he focused his attention out the window at his car. Finally, he said, "I'm moving my car. It's too close to the others." He left the table and moved the car to the back of the parking lot, returned, and they resumed their conversation. But, continuing his gaze out the window, he now noticed that the parking lot was next to a school where children were playing ball. "They're going to hit my car!" he exclaimed, rushing from the restaurant to move it once again. By the end of the lunch, my friend wished her coworker had never bought this beautiful car.

Future Generations

One thing you need to consider if you have a problem dealing with possessions is the example you're setting for your children and grandchildren. If they see you buying on impulse, pulling out your charge card when you see something you want, spending beyond your means, they will see how easy it is and will more than likely walk in the same path when they leave home.

One mother was concerned when she saw the number of gifts her daughter had requested at stores where she registered for her upcoming wedding. Then, while cleaning the house for out-of-state company who would be coming, the mother moved out a grandfather clock. Taped to the back she found a list *she* had made before her own wedding. The list was titled, "Needs and Greeds." She found it was true that the apple doesn't fall far from the tree.

CREDIT CARDS

If compulsive buying and overuse of credit cards is your problem, the following hints may help.

- *Cut up all cards but one to use only in an emergency.* Restrict the use of this card to such things as unexpected house or car repairs, or medical bills, not the monthly department store sale.
- *Leave your card at home when you go shopping.* This helps you avoid impulse buying. It is also easier to follow the next principle.
- *Give yourself at least a 24-hour waiting period before making a large purchase.* In doing this, many times you'll find that you really don't need that item after all or your desire for it has disappeared.

One friend told me that she puts an item in her cart, and after thirty minutes or so, she puts it back. "It is mine for a while, but then I decide I don't need it after all," she says.

I went shopping with a friend one day, who was looking for a dining room set. She found one on sale, but wasn't sure if it was the right color or if it would fit in her dining room. "Why don't you sleep on it?" I asked her. "You can measure the size when you get home."

"If I wait, I won't buy it," she replied, "and I want it."

The salesclerk took the box to the car for her (it had to be assembled), but it didn't fit in the backseat. A couple parked nearby with a pick-up truck offered to take it to her home. She accepted the offer and paid them ten dollars.

The next day, she called me. "It's the wrong color and it's too big," she lamented. "I wish I had waited." She then paid her son ten dollars to take it back to the store. Just a good example that the 24-hour rule does work.

- *Cancel mail order catalogs.* One by one they make their way into your mailbox, and in leafing through the pages, you see this gadget or that one that you just have to have, and off goes your order through the mail or on the Internet. The item arrives and ends up on a pantry shelf or is set out at the next garage sale. Solution: Don't order right away. I've gone through these catalogs and torn out pages of things I thought I wanted, but when it came time to order, I found I didn't need them after all.
- *Pay cash for everything.* It's easy to hand over a credit card since you can't see the total adding up on your monthly statement. But when you see five- and ten-dollar bills leaving your wallet, it hurts.
- *Save unexpected income for unexpected purchases.* It's amazing how much you can save if you drop all your change or coupon money into a jar at the end of each day. (Just this week, I turned in more than fifty dollars in change at the grocery store.) Then, when your child is invited to a birthday party or you see an

especially good sale, you can reach for your jar instead of your card.
• *If you do charge, keep a record.* I heard of one woman who kept a credit card ledger similar to a checking account ledger. She wrote down her purchases, but instead of subtracting as she would a check, she added each purchase in the ledger, which gave her an up-to-date balance of her account. This eliminated an end-of-month shock when the bill arrived.

> *My riches consist not in the extent of my possessions,*
> *but in the fewness of my wants.* (Joseph Brotherton)

• *Don't expect to change overnight.* It has been said that it takes twenty-one days to break a habit. If the task of changing your spending habits seems too overwhelming for you, select one of these suggestions and work on it, then go on to the next one. Remember, you didn't develop this addiction overnight so don't expect to solve the problem overnight.
• *Don't depend on possessions to bring you happiness.* Make a list of the things you enjoy that don't cost money: a compliment from your husband or child, finishing a job you've been putting off, a letter or email from a friend. Concentrating on these pleasures, you'll soon realize you don't need that plastic credit card to bring you contentment. You can experience the real freedom of letting go.

CHAPTER 5

LETTING GO OF THE HURTS IN YOUR LIFE

Our teenage daughter stormed into the house. "I'm not having anything to do with 'Marlene' again."

"What's wrong?" I asked. I listened as Janet poured out a litany of complaints against her friend.

"You need to understand where she's coming from." I reminded her of Marlene's background: She had run away from home in another state, and had moved in with her grandma who was threatening to kick her out.

"Mom," Janet interrupted me. "I don't want to understand her. I just want to be mad at her."

Too often we react the same way when we've been hurt by someone, especially someone we trust. This person may have come from a dysfunctional family. They may be struggling with health or financial problems, or do not have a relationship with Jesus Christ. But we don't take that into consideration; we just want to stay mad at them, carry a grudge, and refuse to forgive them.

Someone once said that unforgiveness is like drinking poison, hoping it will harm the other person. Lynda Dallyn, director of clinical social work at Chandler (Arizona) Regional and Mercy Gilbert medical centers says, "The act of forgiveness is a gift to yourself that allows you the opportunity to take back personal power that you have given to another person or situation over time."[1]

The FREEDOM of *Letting Go*

Shortly after my first letting go experience (saying good-bye to my mother eleven years after she died), I had lunch with a friend who inadvertently let slip something that a mutual friend had said about me. A few weeks before, these words would have haunted me and I would have cried myself to sleep night after night. However, that day, as we separated and I walked to my car in the parking lot, these thoughts ran through my mind:

Maybe she didn't really say that. Maybe my friend misunderstood. If so, that's not my problem.

Maybe she did say it, but she didn't mean it. If so, that's not my problem.

Maybe she did say it and she did mean it, but I know it's not true. Again, it's not my problem, so Lord, I'm leaving it in your hands.

That was more than fifteen years ago, and I have never confronted the person who supposedly said the words, nor have I repeated them to anyone else who knew her. On that day, walking to the car, I realized I had really won my victory over the past.

> *I refuse to be trapped in the past ... It is my choice to forgive, to let you go. You will no longer hold a bitter place in my heart. I'm willing to forgive so that I can be free.* (T. Suzanne Eller)

Victor Frankl, a German/Jewish doctor, was arrested during World War II by the Gestapo, placed in prison, and interrogated by the Nazi secret police under bright lights for hours at a time. They took every one of his possessions, even his wedding band. Frankl said, "I went through many senseless tortures from the hands of the Nazi policemen. I realized that I had only one thing left — the power to choose my own attitude, and I could choose bitterness or forgiveness." He chose forgiveness![2]

Most of us have never gone through what Victor Frankl experienced, but we've all had our share of hurts. A family member turned against us because of a misunderstanding. A friend told lies about us behind our back. A coworker took credit and even received a promotion or a bonus for an idea or project that was ours.

Jean Harder, in her booklet, *Bound by Unforgiveness,* writes, "Perhaps you say, 'I've already forgiven everyone.' If this is true, I challenge you to test your forgiveness by considering the following questions:

- Does the memory of a confrontation still hurt?
- Are you angry at circumstances?
- Is it still hard to look at that person or their picture?
- Do you fear meeting them somewhere?
- Are you still tormented by what happened between you?
- Do you inwardly long for revenge or to tell them off?
- Do you totally lack feeling where a person is concerned?
- Can you face that one just as if he/she had never hurt you?
- Does hearing nice comments about that person cause the old hurt to return?
- Do you become angry when you talk about a past hurt?[3]

One of the greatest stories of forgiveness I have ever heard is told in my friend Kitty Chappell's book, *I Can Forgive If I Want to — Forgiving the Unforgivable* (formerly *Sins of a Father*). Kitty, her mom, and siblings suffered terrifying abuse at the hands of Kitty's father. She was born into an environment of violence, experienced the pain of abuse, and the ravages of rage and resentment. Even after becoming a Christian, Kitty felt she could never forgive her father, especially after he attempted to murder her mother. When someone asked, "Have you forgiven your father?" it infuriated her and agitated her for months with gut-wrenching anger and bitterness until she realized she indeed needed to forgive him. The problem was, she didn't want to. In desperation, she asked God to give her the power to forgive. When she did, God empowered her to experience true freedom. While her story begins with the horror of a child born into abuse, it ends with hope, for it is a story not just about surviving, but about overcoming.[4]

> *It is wonderful what God can do with a broken heart if He can get all the pieces.* (E. Stanley Jones)

It is not easy to forgive. Christ said for us to forgive seventy-times-seven. Does this mean we have to forgive someone four-hundred ninety times? Not necessarily. It simply means to keep on forgiving others or, as the apostle Paul says, "Forgive as the Lord forgave you." (Colossians 3:13)

Bill and Pam Farrel, in their book, *Every Marriage Is a Fixer-Upper,* give several ways to work through the process of forgiveness:

- I forgive (name of person) for (offense that was committed).
- I admit that what was done was wrong.
- I do not expect (name of person) to make up for what he or she has done. Instead, I will define him or her as someone who needs just as much grace in life as I do ...
- I will not manipulate (name of person) with what he or she has done.
- I will not allow what has happened to stop my personal growth.[5]

Because we're human, all too often we may forgive, but we refuse to forget. Writer and former editor, Wightman Weese, tells of an incident when his wife was a child and an argument broke out between her and her younger sister. Tired of hearing them argue, their father shouted, "Hey you two! Bury the hatchet."

"Okay," her sister said, and then whispered, "But I'm gonna leave the handle sticking out."

A Sunday school teacher instructed her students to get a clear plastic bag and a sack of potatoes. Then, for every person they refused to forgive, they had to take a potato, write on it the name of the person and the date, and put the potato in the plastic bag. Then she told the students to carry this bag of potatoes with them everywhere for one whole week. They had to keep it at their bedside every night, in the car, next to their desk at work and so on.

The hassle of lugging that bag around with them made it clear what a weight they were carrying spiritually. Also, the condition of the potatoes deteriorated into a nasty slime, which helped them appreciate the price they paid for holding on to their hurts.

So the next time we just can't seem to forgive someone, we should ask ourselves, "Isn't my bag heavy enough?" We need to empty our sack before it gets too heavy and slimy. Better yet, we don't even have to put any potatoes in it. We can consciously and intentionally forgive in the same way that the Lord has forgiven us.[6]

How often have you heard someone say, "I'm not one to hold a grudge, but ... " and then they repeat a hurt that was done to them years ago? Malcolm Smith, in his book, *Forgiveness*, says,

> "We find some perverse joy in licking old wounds. We return to the hurts again and again, reliving them in a movie we play in the theater of our minds ... a movie in which we are the stars. We see ourselves abused, wronged — but oh so right. Every time we play this movie in our imagination, we bear again what each person said or didn't say, what was done and how it was done. We cling to our memories because, in our

darkened minds, we believe that if we forget, the one who hurt us may go free! ... Bitterness arises from the belief that the person who hurt us owes us and must somehow pay us back.[7]

FORGIVING ISN'T FORGETTING

When you forgive someone, you are not saying that what they did never happened, and it doesn't mean you have forgotten it. One pastor said, "Forgiving is remembering and still forgiving."

Sometimes we don't want to forgive because we'd rather keep on playing the part of a martyr, basking in self-pity, continually telling others how badly we've been hurt. We talk to everyone, except the person who caused us the hurt.

Some of the hardest hurts to forgive, shared earlier in Kitty Chappell's book, are hurts we suffered in childhood. I had a very godly mother, yet, to this day, I remember two hurtful things she said to me when I was young. I'm sure she was under a great deal of stress, raising three children as a single mother on income from babysitting and ironing. If I had mentioned these words to her later, she probably wouldn't have remembered them and would have been shocked that she had even said them. But it's as one friend told me, "If you say ninety-nine positive things about me and one negative, I'll remember the negative."

It is difficult to forget childhood hurts and abuse, but God can give us the power to forgive — not necessarily to set the other person free, but to set us free as shown in the following story a friend shared with me.

"As far back as I can remember, my father has been an alcoholic. He came home from World War II with a monkey on his back, depressed and addicted to alcohol. He and my mother were married in 1945, and twelve years later, they had five children. I was the oldest.

"My father worked several jobs to provide food, shelter and clothes for his family, but at least twice a week he would go to the local bar to drink away his sorrows. He was a mean drunk — verbally and physically — and my mother took the brunt of his anger. She put up with his abuse for fifty-one years before God took her to heaven on her seventieth birthday.

"Her death hit me very hard. With her loss, all those years of abuse came rushing into my heart and the big question of 'what if' came into my mind. What if she had been treated better and didn't have to live with so much stress all her life? Would she have died so soon?

"After eight months of heavy grief, I went to church on Mother's Day. I sat there and cried through the entire service, asking God to help me forgive my father and fill my heart with joy once again. By the end of the service, and after many people came up to me to see if I needed prayer, I felt as if the burden had been lifted.

"Since then I have forgiven my father and have even learned to respect him again. He is now eighty-five years old. He has lung problems, and has also had to have his lower left leg amputated. He is truly sorry for how he treated my mom and hopes to go to heaven to see her again."

Some people believe that if they forgive someone, they must resume the relationship. However, June Hunt reminds us that forgiveness is not the same as reconciliation.

- Forgiveness can take place with only one person; reconciliation requires at least two people.
- Forgiveness is a free gift to the one who has broken trust; reconciliation is a restored relationship based on restored trust.

- Forgiveness is extended even if it is never, ever earned; reconciliation is offered to the offender because it has been earned.
- Forgiveness is unconditional, regardless of a lack of repentance; reconciliation is conditional based on repentance.[8]

If we would show ourselves to be true sons and daughters of God, then we must act like Him in this matter of forgiveness. Unlike our heavenly Father, though, we often find ourselves totally unwilling to seek reconciliation with those who have injured us. We are all for the fact that God was faithful to lovingly search us out when we had turned from Him, but when it comes time for us to reach out to our offenders, that's an entirely different matter. (John McLaughlin)

I found this to be true several years ago when I returned to my hometown for a visit. Having some free time one afternoon, the thought popped into my mind to visit a childhood friend who I heard was sick, but I rebelled against the thought, remembering how that person had cruelly hurt me when I was a teenager. I felt I had forgiven her, but every time I heard her name, those memories returned.

The thought persisted, however, and after getting her address from a mutual friend, I found myself knocking at her door. After reminding her who I was (we hadn't seen each other in more than twenty years) and sharing some family news, I asked if I could pray with her.

"I'd appreciate that," she said.

I began to pray, and after only a few words, I felt her hand slip into mine. Finishing the prayer, I was surprised to see tears running down her cheeks. Somehow, I felt in those moments, she knew her actions of the past had been forgiven.

I walked out of her house that day with a heavy weight lifted off my shoulders. And that, my friend, is freedom!

CHAPTER 6

LETTING GO OF YOUR CHILDREN

"I'll never be an interfering mother-in-law," I promised myself after my daughter married. I thought I'd carried out that promise until, one morning, I woke up thinking of a dilemma they faced.

If I were them, I thought, *I'd* ... I stopped, realizing what I was doing. Then I thought of all the times I had said those very words to them. Or, *If I was in your place, I'd* ... or, I *think you should* ... or, *Why don't you* ... ?

The next time I saw them, I apologized. "If you catch me doing that again, just tell me to 'butt out.'" (A look of relief passed over my son-in-law's face.)

It is difficult to let go of our children, no matter what their stage of life. In her article "Old Enough to Know Better," Marian Edelman Borden says, "While it's hard to keep our opinions to ourselves, there comes a point when an adult child has to make decisions for himself — even if they're not the choices we would make for him."[1]

I always prided myself on being there for my young children. Whenever they argued with a friend, I urged them to apologize, no matter who was at fault. I stepped in to head off school problems. And when they faced important decisions, I advised them which path to take. I was what is called a "helicopter parent," hovering overhead to check on my children's every move to make sure they didn't do something wrong. I never gave them a chance to fail so they could learn from their mistakes.

Our children were adolescents before I realized I had been there for them too much. I made them into what one friend termed "emotional cripples." Thankfully, I realized this soon enough not to carry it into their adulthood.

Lysa TerKeurst, in her book, *Am I Messing Up My Kids?*, came to this same realization. She says,

> "I think this is why I am so mentally spent by the end of the day. My mind is constantly on the go where my kids are concerned … Mostly this happens when I hear of bad things happening to other children — a terrible car accident, a brain tumor, a heart defect, a drowning, a child choking — this list of what-if's goes on and on. No wonder I'm so tired … "

She goes on to say,

> "The reality is that God has assigned a certain number of days to our children, and nothing we do or don't do will add to that number."[2]

> *Mothering*
> *Watching their first steps*
> *as they bravely*
> *walk toward you,*
> *ready to catch them*
> *if they should fall.*
> *Watching them grow up,*
> *and confidently walk away,*

Donna Clark Goodrich

still holding them
ever so gently
in your heart,
and ready to catch them
with your prayers.
—Sharon Dyer

Letting Go Starts Young

Letting go of our children can start young, perhaps even before their birth. I can remember, to my shame, the glib statements I used to make when someone I knew suffered a miscarriage. "That's God's way of taking care of a baby that wouldn't have been right." Or, "Don't feel bad. You can have more children."

Then it happened to our daughter. From the time we found out Janet was pregnant, we ate, slept, and dreamt of that baby. I shopped the infant departments at the mall, picking up things that would go for a boy or a girl. Then a car accident ended her dream and we grieved for what might have been. (She actually grieved twice because the week the baby was due, she began receiving congratulatory letters and samples of baby products, as the obstetrician had sold her name and address to manufacturers.)

Illness

We may have to let go of a child in other ways.

When Janet was born, she possessed a shrill scream that the doctor said was caused by colic. The scream continued into her eighth month when a specialist finally diagnosed her with kidney problems. Then she spent her first Christmas in the hospital with pneumonia. She continued to have problems and ended up back in the hospital a few months later.

During this stay, a friend called me and read me part of an article on cystic fibrosis. I called our doctor. "That sounds like Janet's symptoms," I told him.

"That's what we're testing her for," he replied, adding, "I doubt if she'll live long enough to go to kindergarten."

That night, my husband and I prayed, "Lord, if You aren't going to heal Janet, then it's okay if You take her. It's too hard for us to see her this sick all the time."

When I returned to the hospital the next day, the doctor was in Janet's room. I knew they had performed another test that morning and I was anxious to learn the results. The doctor's words brought tears to my eyes. "We took the last test this morning," he said. "Based on the results of the other tests, it should have turned out positive, but it was negative. Then we went back and reran the other tests, which had been positive earlier, and this time they were also negative. Someone higher than me was looking out for her," he admitted.

I rushed to the telephone to call my husband and share the good news. Later, we learned that students at the seminary he attended had called their home churches all across the United States asking for prayer for our precious one-year-old.

I do not understand God's ways in these situations, as I realize that many children die in spite of thousands of prayers. I just know that, in our hearts, we were willing to let go if God chose to take our baby. We also learned during this time to trust God and lean on Him, no matter what the outcome.

To relinquish your children does not mean to abandon them ... It means to give them back to God, and in so doing to take your hands off ... It means to release those controls that arise from needless fears or from selfish ambitions. (John White)

School Years

We let go of our children on the first day of kindergarten. That's also a scary time. Now they're not only out of our sight all day, but out of our influence. Someone else will be guiding them and teaching them the majority of the day. This is one of our early steps in the letting go process. Max Lucado describes this day beautifully:

> "For four lightning-fast years, she'd been ours and ours alone. And now that was all going to change.
>
> "We'd put her to bed last night as our 'girl' — exclusive property of Mommy and Daddy. Mommy and Daddy read to her, taught her, listened to her. But beginning today, someone else would, too.
>
> "Until today, it was Mommy and Daddy who wiped away the tears and put on the Band-Aids. But beginning today, someone else would, too …
>
> "Her world was this house — her room, her toys, her swing set. Today her world would expand. She would enter the winding halls of education — painting, reading, calculating … becoming.
>
> "I didn't want to wake her. Not because of the school. It's a fine one. Not because I don't want her to learn. Heaven knows I want her to grow, to read, to mature. Not because she doesn't want to go. School has been all she could talk about for the last week!
>
> "No, I didn't want to wake her up because I didn't want to give her up."[3]

The Teen Years

You might not think adolescence is part of the letting go stage, but it is. It's letting go of that once innocent, pliable child. Suddenly,

The FREEDOM of *Letting Go*

you're faced with a moody, unpredictable stranger. Perhaps you feel like Jessica Martin's description of this new person in her home.

> "You break your neck for your friends,
> but you don't seem to care about your own family."
> Lord, I've spoken those words so often to my teenager.
> They're true!
> When friends call, she'll drop everything for them,
> but she won't even bother if I need help.
> I get angry and frustrated — and hurt.
> It's hard to see others take priority in my daughter's life.
> I know this is part of growing up.
> Her life can no longer revolve around us.
> Soon she'll establish a home of her own.
> Help me, Lord, to let go.
> Help me not to demand
> what my daughter can no longer give.
> And free me from wanting to protect her.
> Sure, her friends may let her down,
> but she has to learn that for herself.
> I cannot make decisions for her.
> I cannot put her in a box.
> But I can trust you to be with us both
> through these difficult years.
> Lord, let us emerge more than mother and daughter.
> Help us to become the best of friends. ©*1985 by Jessica Martin*

THE EMPTY NEST

It's more difficult to let go when your young adult leaves home for the first time, whether for college or for another reason, and you're facing an empty nest. In a devotional published in *The Secret Place*, Emily Akin writes,

> "Suddenly, it happened to me. I was an empty-nester. In my struggle with my new role in life, I drew strength from the third chapter of Ecclesiastes … 'There is a time for everything, and a season for every activity under heaven.'
>
> "I found little comfort in the advancing of the seasons of life. It just reminded me that my life was almost over. My children didn't need me any more … As I studied further, I realized that, although my time of being needed every day by my own children was over, I could 'do good while I live' by volunteering in the community and in the church.
>
> An empty nest does not equal an empty life. It can be full and rewarding with serving others at the center. Indeed, God has 'made everything beautiful in its time.'"

I love how C. Roy Angell describes a mother eagle helping her young ones leave the nest.

> "The ceremony began with the destruction of the nest. The old eagle tore up the nest and threw the pieces over the cliff. Then she took the little eaglet on her broad back and, circling, carried him high into the sun. Then she tilted her wings and slid him off into space.
>
> "Fluttering, screeching, screaming, he drifted down. The old eagle circled around him. Long before the eaglet reached the sharp crags and rocks below, she glided under him and caught him on her strong wings. Two or three times she repeated this, as if to say, 'See, you cannot fall, for underneath are the everlasting wings.'"[4]

Sometimes, however, even after our children have left the nest, we want to hang on to them. We bail them out of trouble, fill up their gas tank, and take out a credit card in our name to help them pay their bills.

Many years ago, I went with a friend to a retreat center to spend a few days and do some writing. Sitting with the other guests one night at dinner, I shared with them the many times God had provided for our family after my father left. My mother supported the three children still at home by babysitting and taking in ironings — and a lot of prayer.

"Our kids haven't had that experience of trusting God for their needs like we did," my friend commented. Then light dawned and she confessed, "That's because my husband and I have been God for them. We've met so many of their needs, they haven't had to depend on God."

It's especially difficult to let go of our children when we see them making destructive choices. We want to rush in and rescue them, but when we hover over our grown kids, we send a message to them that they can't do anything on their own. They will soon lose all sense of self-confidence, believing they're incapable of making a right decision.

Our Mt. Moriah

I often questioned God's purpose in asking Abraham to sacrifice his only son. As I read the passage over again one day (Genesis 22:1-19), several new thoughts came to me. In verses 2 and 3, God commanded Abraham to take his only son Isaac to Moriah and sacrifice him there as a burnt offering. We read that, early the next morning, Abraham got up and did exactly what God told him to do. I wonder if I would have been so obedient if God had asked me for my only child.

A phrase in verse 4 — "on the third day" — also brought questions to my mind. What did father and son talk about during that three-day journey? What was in Abraham's heart?

In verse 5, Abraham said to his servants, "Stay here ... while I and the boy go over there. We will worship and then we will come back to you." Why did he say that they both would return? Did he have faith from past experiences that the Lord would provide?

Then in verse 13: "Abraham looked up and there in a thicket he saw a ram caught by its horns." The ram must have been there all the time, but God did not allow Abraham to see it until He had tested his faithfulness.

This passage of Scripture not only proves that God's timing is always perfect, but also that He will take care of our children if we let go of them and leave them in His hands.

Others in the Bible also were called to give their children into God's keeping. Hannah prayed fervently for a child — to the point that Eli, the priest, thought she was drunk. Finally, her prayers were answered and God gave her a son. You would think that after all the years of being childless, she would keep this son close to her side as long as she could. But no. Remembering her promise to the Lord, she gave up her most precious possession — her Samuel — and allowed him to be raised in the Temple. "So now I give him to the LORD. For his whole life he will be given over to the LORD." (1 Samuel 1:28)

We read also about Jochebed. When Pharaoh ordered all the male babies born to the Jews to be drowned in the Nile, Jochebed hid baby Moses for three months. Then she placed him in an ark of bulrushes and put it by the river's bank where Pharaoh's daughter found him. But that wasn't the end of the story. In God's providence, He allowed Jochebed to nurse the baby she had put into the ark.

The FREEDOM of *Letting Go*

As a teenager, I pulled a Scripture verse out of a Promise Box one day that read, "I shall give thee the heathen for thine inheritance." From that I concluded that God wanted me to be a missionary — to Africa, of course. Wasn't that where all missionaries went? My mother was thrilled, as it was her dream that one of her children would be a minister or a missionary.

Later, I realized that this was only a personal desire, not a true calling. Then, a year later, a dream came true when our denominational publishing house offered me a job as secretary to the book editor. My mother wasn't too happy about this, however. It seemed a mission field thousands of miles away excited her, but not Kansas City — seven-hundred fifty miles away. The Sunday after I left, our pastor preached a sermon on standing in other people's way, and my mother wrote me and asked for my forgiveness.

I did not understand her pain of losing our close companionship until many years later when my daughter and newly ordained son-in-law had the chance to take a church a thousand miles away. "No, Lord," I sobbed. "I don't want them to go that far and take our two granddaughters."

I spent many agonizing hours on my knees that week, and finally managed to put the family in God's hands. Then I wrote my daughter a poem, closing with the words:

> It's not my approval you're needing
> When you stand before the throne —
> But your heavenly Father's favor
> As He says, "My child, well done."
>
> His is the voice you must listen to —
> His is the path you must take —

His are the steps you must follow
If souls will be won for His sake.

I'd rather you be miles away
And following His command,
Then to stay here — because we're near
And lose blessings from His hand.

So as I dedicated you to God
When you were an infant so small,
I now give you back to Him again
That you may obey His call.

Two years after I wrote the above poem for my daughter, my son-in-law did indeed take a church in Oklahoma, 1,000 miles away. But because I had surrendered them to the Lord earlier, it made it much easier. Though we miss them immensely, I thank God every day that they are in His will and serving Him.

In a Jewish wedding, both sets of parents accompany the bride and groom down the aisle, in essence saying, "We're taking our hands off. You're on your own now."

BEFORE THEY SAY "I DO"

At the beginning of this chapter I shared how I had to stop offering advice to my daughter and her new husband when they were first married. However, what if your son or daughter begins dating someone you disapprove of? This happened to my friend Sharon.

"Anxious to meet our sixteen-year-old daughter Julie's boyfriend, we invited him over for dinner. Our hearts sank when he appeared wearing sagging black pants with chains hanging from them, and a black t-shirt. *It's what's inside that matters,* we chided ourselves.

"Over dinner, we learned Justin came from a non-Christian, broken home with addiction problems. Though concerned for our daughter, we feared forbidding her to date Justin would only fuel her determination to do so. We chose to let the relationship run its course, sure it wouldn't last long. We were wrong.

"The next year saw rebellion in Julie. She became distant and began hanging out with a rough crowd. Unfortunately, afraid for her and her future, we often demonstrated our fear in anger and poor parenting skills.

"After Julie ran away one night, we found her, but couldn't convince her to return home. Instead, she stayed at my parents' house. Once, she stopped by to get a few things from her room. I prayed she'd stay, but when she didn't, fresh grief washed over me. 'I've done all I can for her, God. I've taught her Your ways and loved her more than life itself. I don't know what else to do, so I'm leaving her in Your hands.' Instantly, relief replaced my grief and I knew Julie was in the best place possible.

"A few days later, she came home — for good.

"Not long after, Julie revealed that she was pregnant. Heartbroken, we determined to stand by her, secretly thinking Justin would probably drop out of the picture after the novelty of a newborn wore off. Wrong again.

"Julie graduated from high school seven months pregnant. Our first grandchild — a boy — was born and the relationship with our daughter improved. We gave thanks for our renewed, warm relationship. Justin graduated the following year, and he and Julie married. My husband and I never stopped praying for them, especially for Justin's salvation.

"One day I got a call from Julie. 'I'm bringing a new Christian to church.'"

"'Really? Who?'"

"Justin."

"Praise, relief, thankfulness and love all mixed together and welled out in tears. God answered our prayers!

"Today, Justin and Julie are a strong Christian couple with four beautiful boys and a darling girl. They're wonderful parents, possessing wisdom beyond their years. I couldn't have handpicked a better son-in-law for us, or husband and father for Julie and their boys. We're so thankful."

The situation doesn't always have a happy ending, like the one above. Sometimes, after praying with our son or daughter and sharing our concerns with them, if they are still determined to go ahead with the wedding, we need to accept the relationship and the new son- or daughter-in-law, knowing that any negative reaction can only cause bitterness. If the marriage fails, rather than have an "I-told-you-so" attitude, we need to be there for them to help pick up the pieces.

When They Stray from Your Teachings

In his book, *The Wounded Parent — Coping with Parental Discouragement,* Guy Greenfield writes:

> "The words *hurt, angry, frustrated, confused, rejected, offended, embarrassed, used, abused, disappointed, unappreciated* and *resentful* describe how parents may feel when their children go

astray morally and spiritually. Parents ask each other, 'How could this happen to us? ... Where did we go wrong?'"

Greenfield said the day he and his wife both accepted that he wasn't Superman and his wife wasn't Wonder Woman "was a day a heavy burden was lifted."[5]

When our son was a toddler, he had a habit of holding his breath if he didn't get his own way. Terrified that he would pass out, I expressed my fears to my doctor. "Just let him go," he said. "If he passes out, he'll start breathing again automatically."

I recall as though it were yesterday, the first time I did this (and, incidentally, the last time he tried it). Kicking and screaming, his face grew red as he held his breath. I walked away and he *did* pass out — but only for an instant.

Years later, I had to let go of him again. This was shortly after I let go of my mother, and I was learning new lessons every day. My husband and I were both in bed when our son came in and asked us to give him a ride to the house of a girl he had dated earlier, much to our disapproval. "I'll take him," my husband said.

In days past, I would have stayed awake, tossing and turning, wondering what was happening. Instead, that night, I prayed, "Lord, watch over him. If he does anything he shouldn't, let him know that it'll be over his mother's prayer." And I went to sleep.

When I awoke the next morning, I noticed our son's bedroom door was closed. *That's strange,* I thought. *It was open when he left.* A few minutes later, he came out of his room.

"What happened?" I asked.

"She wasn't there," he replied. "I had to walk home."

Relief, and then thankfulness, came over me — thankfulness that I had been able to leave him in God's hands and get a good night's sleep. Remembering this night, I often think of a pastor's sermon on the Prodigal Son. "The father didn't run after his son," he said, "but he was waiting with open arms when he returned."

*****

As we've seen in this chapter, it is truly difficult to let go of our children, but not so much when we realize that they aren't ours to begin with. As Pam Farrel notes, "We do not own our children. God has lent them to us, entrusted them to us and our job as parents is to pass God's wisdom, God's perspective and God's instruction on to them, all the while holding them with an open-handed attitude."[6]

And all God's parents said, "Amen!"

CHAPTER 7

LETTING GO OF HEALTH ISSUES

WHEN YOUR HUSBAND IS ILL

"Things just aren't the same as they used to be. I know it. Can't you realize it?" The veins stood out on my husband's neck, and his hands shook as he shouted the words. Our three children peered around the corner of the kitchen and stared, wide-eyed, wondering what was going on.

I, too, was shocked. I had simply asked about plans for a vacation this year and my husband exploded. This wasn't the easygoing, good-natured man I married almost twenty-six years ago. A stranger now stood before me. Well, on second thought, not *really* a stranger. Gary had changed since that night two years before when he had suffered a massive heart attack at forty-eight. (This scared both of us, as his mother had died of a heart attack at the age of fifty-one.)

Gary spent four days in intensive care, and another six days in cardiac care, before returning home. Tests showed no permanent damage and he didn't need surgery. The doctor cleared him to return to work.

In the meantime, however, he developed another health problem diagnosed as Crohn's disease. That, combined with his arthritis and diabetes, led to an early retirement a few months later.

Before his heart attack, Gary and I had looked forward to his retirement. We planned to visit baseball parks and friends throughout the United States — our "golden years." But due to his many illnesses, his retirement was anything but golden.

At the beginning, we went for walks together and Gary helped with the housework. Eventually, however, he settled into a routine of watching television from early morning to midnight. He lived in his recliner, even for meals. I ran my own business in a downtown office and dreaded returning home after a long day to my husband's growing depression. Tension built, which eventually led to the above outburst.

I knew something had to change, so the next morning I sat down at the dining room table and poured out my heart to God. Following are some ideas that helped make our home a more loving and peaceful place to live. If you're a caregiver for your husband, perhaps they'll help you too.

- *Your husband is still the head of the house.* Respect him. After my husband retired, I found myself making more of the household decisions. I called repairmen. I handled the checkbook. Once I realized that this made him feel even less useful than he already felt, I gave the checkbook back to him. He paid the bills and balanced the monthly statement. He also thrived on making phone calls to straighten out various problems on insurance and other household difficulties.
- *If you're working, involve your spouse in your work.* Because I had begun my business at home, my husband knew many of my customers, so I could share my work with him. I also began asking his advice on the business. I discovered that he could look at my problems from a different point of view and offer creative solutions.
- *Return home in a positive mood.* When I arrived home, I shared the good happenings of the day, saving any negative news until

The FREEDOM of *Letting Go*

after dinner or for the weekend. I remembered how I wanted him to come through the door when I was in the house all day awaiting his return.

- *Make a list of things you want him to do.* I made a list of jobs and divided them into columns he could do, I could do or the children could do. Some we did together.
- *Appreciate what he does and thank him.* I recall nagging him several days in a row about vacuuming the living room floor. One night I came home and automatically griped, "When are you going to vacuum?"

"I did it yesterday," he replied. I was so used to finding fault, I hadn't noticed.

- *Forget the past.* Unemployment is especially hard for men. My husband felt guilty that he couldn't work and support his family. I probably never really knew the depth of his discouragement when I walked out the door every morning. Our lives would never be the same. As he shouted out to me that one day, he knew it, and I needed to accept it and plan our future realistically.
- *Be content with less.* I learned to be satisfied with the cleanliness of the house, even though it wasn't always up to my standards (actually, sometimes it looked better). I became content with shorter vacations closer to home. We ate out less often because he had meals ready when I came home. And I let my husband know I was content. I had nearly lost him. Material things could now take second place.
- *Plan activities for the two of you.* Even though we could no longer take lengthy vacations, we still needed to spend time alone as husband and wife. One evening I prepared a candlelight meal, using our best china. Other activities included going to baseball games or taking a lunch to the park or a roadside table.

- *Set aside a time for devotions or meditation.* Depression easily overwhelms a person with disabilities, and one person's bad mood can permeate the entire family. It is good to set aside a time to share a passage from the Bible or a devotional book with the family, and also pray together. Everyone benefits from this.
- *Tell your husband — often — that you love him.* Remember, only your husband's body is disabled. He is still a vital, essential part of your life and needs to be reminded of this often. Let him know every day that he is loved, not because of what he is, but because of who he is — a man after God's own heart.

Talking with many friends and relatives who deal with a spouse's chronic disease, I found that they, too, have discovered that the experience can either weaken or strengthen a marriage relationship.

A Turning Point

When I first began going through my letting go process, one of the things I knew I had to let go of was my husband's health. At that time he had myriad diseases, including diabetes, heart trouble, and several bone diseases.

Every time he came home from the doctor, I would ask him, "What did the doctor say?" ... "Are you sure you're telling me everything?" Or I would say, "You don't look very good today. Are you sure you're all right?" (And if he said "yes," I wouldn't believe him.)

One day I said to him, "Honey, I'm letting go of your health. You're an adult and from now on I'm going to trust you to know when and if you need to make a doctor's appointment. I'm not going to nag you any more." (The look of relief on his face was priceless!)

Shortly afterwards, I noticed a sore on his leg that didn't look like it was healing. Just as I opened my mouth to say something, he said, "Don't worry. I've already made an appointment." I couldn't believe it! My husband had actually made a doctor's appointment on his own without my help!

A friend told me recently that she had let go of controlling her husband's weight. "In the past I nagged him about it, and it became worse," she said. "He was dealing with things that I knew nothing about, his eating was out of control and it didn't help that I kept after him. Now I have let go of this problem. It's his — not my — concern. No amount of nagging will make another person toe the line and eat to lose."

WHEN YOUR WIFE IS ILL

It can be especially hard on a husband when his wife is ill. It's one thing if it's a temporary setback such as a surgery or even a broken bone — something that she'll eventually recover from. It's another thing when a wife suffers from a chronic illness, as the husband not only has to take on many of the household chores, he may also have to assume "mothering" duties. He may even — as I had to — have to give up plans for vacations and trips.

CARETAKERS

Just a note here to those who care for a loved one day after day after day. There are many excellent books that deal with this subject, so I won't dwell on this too much except to say, *take time for yourself.* It is easy for a caregiver to also become discouraged. It seems all the attention is focused on the sick person, and you wonder if anyone cares how you are doing.

One day, after my son-in-law was diagnosed with multiple sclerosis, I asked my daughter, "Do you ever get tired of everyone asking how he is, and no one asking how you are?" She burst into tears.

Do something *just for you*. Caring for someone with a chronic illness brings on a lot of stress and you need some space. Have lunch with a friend, or take a leisurely stroll through the mall. Some malls have "walking clubs." Get a partner and lose a few pounds while you chat and relax. If you don't take care of yourself, you won't be much help to the person you're taking care of.

Cathy Messecar, author of *A Still and Quiet Soul: Embracing Contentment,* wrote on The Writer's View Web site:

> "My husband and I have the rare privilege of caring for four elderly parents, all within five miles of our home. We are self-employed with a full, but flexible schedule. With my mother under hospice care, I pared down activities to assist my dad in his caretaking.
>
> "Over the past year, a thought kept surfacing through scripture and meditation until I could no longer ignore the message. While God dwells in the past, and will be in the future, I can only experience His grace at the moment I'm breathing in. I've made this commitment: 'Live in the grace of the moment.'"

When singer and songwriter Janet Paschal was undergoing chemo treatments for breast cancer, she made the following observation:

> "It occurred to me that this disease and its treatment are much worse on the husbands and wives … than it is the person who gets the plastic bracelet or the clean, white blanket. Those wives watched yesterday as the lethal fluids dripped into the plastic lines feeding directly into the veins of the person they married forty years, or two years, ago, knowing only this — that it can

have very negative repercussions and that it may not work. They also know they'll do it again next week or at the next appointment because it is still their best option …

"I thought of how helpless these spouses must be feeling … The doctors offer them percentages and recommendations, but their information is strewn with educated guesses. The only things they know for sure is that this is the person with whom they remember their first kiss, their first house and their days before cancer was in their everyday conversation.

"It was the spouses yesterday who checked to make sure all their bags were retrieved before leaving. It was the spouses who dug for their keys in early preparation and called to let everyone know they were on their way. It was the spouses who took the arms of the patients and led them slowly toward the exit, with a look of quiet resolve and supernatural strength.

"It occurred to me that perhaps these people don't understand how strong they are becoming."[1]

It's Okay to Ask Why

Perhaps the most frequent question asked when a family member suffers, is "Why?" "Why is this happening to me or to my loved one?"

Marion Nelson, in his book, *Why Christians Crack Up*, asks this same question: "Why would God deliberately bring us tribulation, perhaps in the form of a physical or mental disorder, when we are living godly, obedient lives?" Then he answers: "1) To achieve purification of our Christian life (2 Cor. 7:9,11); 2); To produce patience and endurance (Rom. 5:3; Jam. 1:3); 3); To produce humility (2 Cor. 12:7-10); 4); To produce dependence upon God (2 Cor. 1:8-9)."[2]

One writer states, "After a lot of years of living and celebrating and suffering, I do have some convictions in my heart about God's relation to our suffering.

- I know that God is good — I just know it.
- I believe that after Calvary, God has a right to be trusted.
- I believe that when we suffer, God suffers.
- I know that when God himself wanted to achieve the salvation of humankind, He chose to do it through *suffering* ...
- I believe that it is divine love that brings Christ walking quietly into the deepest shadows of my sorrow to meet me there.
- I believe that we are never more precious to our God than when we suffer."[3]

Although we may not understand at the time why God allows certain things in our lives, later we can look back and see His plan. I found this especially true during my mother's last three weeks of life.

For my thoughts are not your thoughts, neither are your ways my ways, saith the LORD. *(Isaiah 55:8)*

"Lord, why have you let Mother linger so long? You know she's ready to go." I prayed these words at two o'clock in the morning in December 1982. Sitting in the tiny, smoke-filled waiting room of the Intensive Care Unit, I thought back over the events of the previous eighteen months: my mother's cancer surgery, the chemo treatments, my eight trips between Arizona and Michigan, and the final surgery that led to the coma in which she now lay.

The week before, the doctor had told me "24-to-48 hours" and I had summoned my brothers and sister who had come — along with some of their children — to be by Mother's bedside. Day after day, we waited and watched. "She quit breathing," someone would say and we'd rush to the cafeteria to get a family member. But by the time we returned, her breathing had resumed.

Exhausted, and needing to return home for a statewide Christian writers' seminar I was leading, I often found myself alone in this little waiting room, praying and questioning God. On this particular night, however, I was not alone for long. A man I guessed to be in his middle sixties made his way into the room, dragging his IV stand beside him. "How are you doing?" I asked him.

"Not too good," he answered in a low voice. "My doctor told me today I have only six months to live."

We chatted for a while. "Elmer" asked why I was there and I told him about my mother.

"How did she handle it when they told her?" he asked me.

I shared with him about her Christian faith, which had sustained her all through the years of raising three children alone on a limited income. I also told him that many people had been praying for her.

"I used to pray," he admitted, "but I don't anymore. It's too late."

"It's never too late," I told him. Reaching into my purse, I took out my New Testament and turned to John 3:16.

"Listen to this verse," I told him. I read the words, putting his name in the appropriate places: "For God so loved Elmer, that he gave his only begotten Son, that [if] Elmer believes in him Elmer shall not perish, but have everlasting life."

Elmer read the verse again, then looked up and asked, "Does that mean there's still a chance for me?"

"That's exactly what it means," I answered. I explained the gospel message simply and then asked if he would like to pray. He bowed his head and repeated the words I said to him. When we finished, he said, simply, "Thank you," and left the room.

The next day, walking down the hall, I looked up and saw Elmer coming toward me. His head erect, he shook my hand and said, "It's okay. I'm not afraid to die now."

Then I knew why God let my mother linger for so long. It was for Elmer's sake.

When It's Your Health

My friend Cindy Scinto has been ill with heart disease for seven years. During that time she has undergone fifty-nine inpatient hospital stays, dozens of procedures, including twenty-eight angioplasties, a number of stents, two open-heart surgeries, a heart transplant, a pancreas transplant, and several rounds of chemotherapies.[4] Six years after the first blockages impaired her heart, she made thirty-six visits to the catheterization lab. Early on in her illness, God gave her the following verses and they kept her steady throughout the dozens of hospital stays and two near-death experiences:

Deal courageously, and the LORD shall be with the good. (2 Chronicles 19:11 KJV)

Do not grieve, for the joy of the LORD is your strength. (Nehemiah 8:10)

After her heart transplant, Cindy wrote, "I feel my heart beating in my chest. It keeps me alive, but somewhere in the deepest part of my soul is another heartbeat that depends on God's redeeming touch. He can get to this spiritual heart only if I let Him." For Cindy, the condition of her spiritual heart and her relationship with God were more important to her than the new physical heart that had been placed within her body.

She went through many times of discouragement when doctors refused to believe her, telling her it "was all in her head," only to realize after testing that something was drastically wrong. But the hardest part for her was not being able to serve in the many ministries at her church. She writes,

> "After each procedure or surgery, I often would chase the dream that I was going to recover completely. Alone one day, I cried and pleaded with God, 'Please heal me so I can serve You once again.'
>
> "For years before my illness, I had been part of many events at church. I scurried from one area to the next — from changing diapers in the nursery to playing flute on the worship team. I wanted it all back. God's reply was precise: 'You are serving Me.'
>
> "I had to rediscover where it was that God wanted me to be and how He wanted me to serve Him."

When people presented "cures" and "healing organizations" for Cindy, she told them,

> "I appreciate your concern, but what is more powerful — a physical healing or a changed heart? God is using me even in my weakness. I am sharing with so many people who are being encouraged by the absolute power of God in my life. If I were to be healed, I would be done. Oh, I would still have my story to tell, but by living it out each day, I can be a very real example of faithful perseverance."

She quotes Tim Hansel, author of *You Gotta Keep Dancin'*, "I had discovered a peace inside the pain."

Cindy even found a way to see the humorous side of her situation. After being on a pacemaker for almost six months, she noticed that one day she felt more lethargic than usual. She went in to see her cardiologist and they checked the pacemaker. It was fine, but the fact was, her heart was no longer beating on its own. The pacemaker had taken over entirely. Cindy thought about that, and then asked her cardiologist to make out a death certificate.

"What for?" he asked in shock.

Cindy replied, "Well, if my heart is no longer beating on its own, then I am actually dead! If you make out a death certificate, I can send it in to my life insurance company and collect my life insurance. I could really use the money now!"

Use This Time to Draw Closer to God

When I broke my wrist in four places (playing racquetball with my son!), I decided, "Now I'll have more time to write." I went through my files and dragged out old manuscripts, did some minor editing, sent them out, and waited for the responses. They came — twelve rejections in one day!

"I quit!" I told my husband, throwing the envelopes on the floor.

Then I sensed a quiet voice within: "I just want you to use this time to get close to Me." I realized that, while I couldn't do housework, type (much), or drive, I could read the Bible and catch up on my pile of Christian books; I could make telephone calls and send cards to shut-ins; and I could pray.

One of my mother's favorite sayings was, "When a person's flat on his back, the only way he can look is up." This is similar to what a hospital roommate told Jill Briscoe: "You think you've been laid aside by illness, but you haven't. You've been called aside for stillness."[5]

The FREEDOM of *Letting Go*

John Ruskin says that, "We need a rest in our lives just as a rest is needed in music." He continues,

> "There is no music in a rest, but there is the making of music in it … God sends a time of forced leisure, sickness, disappointed plans, frustrated efforts and makes a sudden pause in the choral hymn of our lives; and we lament that our voices must be silent … [Rests] are not to be slurred over, not to be omitted, not to destroy the melody, not to change the keynote. If we look up, God Himself will beat the time for us."[6]

Just set aside! It seems a strange procedure,
Just set aside when life was at its best;
There was no choice and service would be sweeter,
Just gently, firmly set aside to rest.

Just set aside! Dear God, I tried to serve Thee,
And thought I played a small important part.
I'm eager still — but what have I to give Thee?
Just set aside, I lean against Thy heart.

Just set aside! I hear Thy sweet voice whisper,
Just set aside that you may come to know
That fuller, richer, still and sweet communion
So often missed when hurrying to and fro.

Just set aside! I'm still impatient, though
I drink with joy the rivers of Thy grace,
Surrounded by Thy love I try to be content
To have glimpsed anew Thy precious face.

Just set aside in holy sweet communion;
Just trusting when I do not understand;
Just set aside perhaps to serve Thee better,
Just waiting in the hollow of Thy hand.
—"Just Set Aside," Alice Mortenson

Good can come out of suffering. At one time in the ministry of Salvation Army commissioner Samuel L. Brengle, a man attempted to kill him by throwing a brick at his head. Brengle survived the attack, but had a long convalescent period during which he wrote articles on the sanctified life. Later, these were placed in a book titled, *Helps to Holiness*. Referring to the earlier incident, his wife said, "Had there been no brick, there would have been no book."[7]

Many of us have read C.S. Lewis' statement that "God whispers to us in our pleasures, speaks in our conscience, but shouts in our pain. It is His megaphone to rouse a deaf world."

God's megaphone spoke to my son-in-law in a Sunday evening service. He had felt a call to the ministry in his teens, but had never followed through. Later in life, his struggle with multiple sclerosis brought him closer to the Lord. He returned to school, and at the age of forty-six, he graduated college, was ordained to the ministry, and accepted his first church. He says, "During my journey, God revealed many things to me and I began to let go of my life and give it all to Him. What I do now is a direct result of His love and grace as He shaped me into a new creature of faith."

One morning a lady in our Bible study made the comment, "I can't thank God *for* my suffering, but I can thank Him *in* my suffering." There's a big difference. It's difficult to thank God for the trials that pierce us to the soul.

Scottish theologian and hymn writer, George Matheson, who

lost his eyesight — and his fiancé — when he was twenty years old, wrote:

> "My God, I have never thanked Thee for my thorns. I have thanked Thee a thousand times for my *roses,* but not once for my *thorns.* I have been looking forward to a world where I shall get compensation for my cross: but I have never thought of my cross as itself a present glory. Teach me the glory of my cross: teach me the value of my thorn. Show me that I have climbed to Thee by the path of pain. Show me that my tears have made my rainbow."[8]

I remember tossing and turning in my hospital bed the night before a serious surgery. I worried about how long the recuperation would take. I worried that if I didn't make it through, who would take care of my husband and our three toddlers? One "what-if" after another echoed through my mind until the words of an old hymn crowded them out:

> "And He walks with me, and He talks with me,
> And He tells me I am His own;
> And the joy we share as we tarry there,
> None other has ever known."[9]

This reminder that I was "His own" gave me peace, and I slept soundly the rest of the night. The surgery — although more difficult than expected — proved successful. More important, however, was the lesson I learned that night, that even while going through physical struggles, He would walk with me and talk with me the rest of my life.

One pastor told of his worry when he was facing a second heart surgery and a lengthy hospital stay. He feared his pastoral career was over. Then God said to him, "It is not your life, it is Mine. It is not your ministerial career, that is Mine too. Those are not your people, they are Mine. That is not your church. It, too, is Mine."

The pastor's reply was, "Dear Lord, if I never preach again, if my congregation goes to another ... I will love and serve You just the same — as long as I live."

When the pastor "let go," God restored to him his complete health, His pulpit, and His people. [10]

Disability is a matter of perception. If you can do just one thing well, you're needed somewhere by someone. (Mobil Oil Corporation ad)

When God Says No

God doesn't always restore our health to us, or our loved ones, however. I wish I had an answer to why God sometimes says no to healing. When I had a lump removed, which turned out to be benign, I wanted to share it one Wednesday night with our church family. Sitting in front of me, however, was a friend I had known for more than twenty-five years. Her lump wasn't benign, and the cancer had spread throughout her body. I kept silent.

Marlene Bagnull had the same experience.

"Several members of a lay-witness team visiting our church spoke joyously of God's healing of loved ones in response to their prayers. I wanted to rejoice with them, but my focus was drawn to a dear friend who was a widow. I hurt inside for her, remembering how she too had prayed for a miracle. Yet the Lord had not chosen to heal her husband. He had died a slow, painful death from cancer.

"I winced as I thought of how the witness of these well-meaning Christians was affecting her and the other bereaved ones in our congregation. I could almost hear in the hushed silence their anguished and unspoken questions: 'Why, Lord? Why didn't you answer my prayers? Didn't I have enough faith? Don't You love me as much as You love these others?'

"I thought of my Lord, and of His deep sensitivity to the feelings of others. 'Come to me, all of you who are tired from carrying heavy loads, and I will give you rest.' (Matthew 11:28 TEV)

"I remembered His promise to the sorrowing, that He would again fill their lives with laughter and joy. (Luke 6:21)

"I realized that His promise was not to save us from life's difficulties, but rather to be with us in them and to work good through them." (Romans 8:28,35-39)[11]

When my husband was in the hospital with a broken hip and other complications, a friend from our church was in the adjoining room. I went over and prayed with her, and her husband came over and prayed with my husband. My husband came home; our friend's wife didn't.

Our entire church prayed for months for our children's minister in her middle forties. A minor stroke led to another, then another, then a heart attack, and soon her two teenage sons were left without a mother. And we asked why? It isn't wrong to ask, "Why?" Someone has said, "Even Christ on the cross asked, 'Why?'"

Stuart and Jill Briscoe, in their article entitled, "When God Says 'NO'," state, "There is no doubt God can grant physical healing. He frequently does. Sometimes He heals through physicians (whom He's gifted) and medications (which He created) ... But these blessed facts should not lead us to assume God will grant healing whenever we ask Him ... Even when our Lord asked to be relieved of the bitter cup in Gethsemane, He ... received the same answer [we sometimes do] — 'No!'"

The Briscoes go on to say that we should avoid thinking we should be healed because we are "more righteous" than other folks. "God's blessings — physical, spiritual, eternal or temporal — are not deserved; they are gifts of His grace."[12]

Cindy Scinto, whose story we shared earlier in this chapter, admits that

> "Divine healing cannot be defined by *Webster's* dictionary nor can it be forced by our will. The answer for healing may not come until God's appointed time. Or the healing may be so different from what we prayed for that we might not recognize it as a healing. God's purpose for healing cannot be limited by our personal desires. The strength we gain by trusting Him to take us through our trials sets an example for others who may be suffering and in need of encouragement."

Conclusion

The most encouraging thought we can carry with us when going through an illness or watching a family member suffer is to know that the Lord is there with us and He understands what we're going through.

> "Now that we know what we have — Jesus, this great High Priest with ready access to God — let's not let it slip through our fingers. We don't have a priest who is out of touch with our reality. He's been through weakness and testing, experienced it all — all but the sin. So let's walk right up to him and get what he is so ready to give. Take the mercy, accept the help." (Hebrews 4:15 MSG)

The FREEDOM of *Letting Go*

Songwriter Dave Clark endured nineteen years of a painful throat disease for which twenty-nine doctors at Mayo Clinic could find no cure — until God stepped in. During his illness he penned the following song:

⌐ I've Been There ⌐

I said Lord I know that You've already taken me
To places that some will never see
And I know that I've been blessed
But Lord I must confess
The journey's almost got the best of me
He said Child I know the miles have got you feeling low
And you wonder how much farther you can go
The pain you feel is real
I know exactly how you feel
And there is only one way I can know

I've been there
I've faced those lonely trials
I've been there
I'm familiar with the miles
So if you're walking through the valley
Of the heartache once again
You're only going where I've already been.

I said Lord it's hard to keep from feeling like I do
When I question why the test you've put me through
Yet in my darkest hour
I've felt a healing power
That only comes from walking close to you

Donna Clark Goodrich

He said Child it's hard to watch the hurt you're going through
And the questions that you ask are nothing new
Sometimes the Father's plan
Is so hard to understand
There've been days that I've felt the same as you.

I've been there
I've faced those lonely trials
I've been there
I'm familiar with the miles
So if you're walking through the valley
Of the heartache once again
You're only going where I've already been.[13]

CHAPTER 8

LETTING GO OF YOUR YOUTH

> *Grow old along with me!*
> *The best is yet to be.*
> *The last of life, for which*
> *the first was made.*
> —Robert Browning

"I can't give you the senior discount on this," the saleswoman told me. "It's already on sale."

"That's fine," I told her. Then, as an afterthought, I asked, "By the way, what's the age for the senior discount here?"

"Sixty-five," she replied.

I was fifty-two!

This incident upset me, but I should have been getting used to it. For several years, waitresses had offered to give me senior discounts at restaurants. "Don't let it bother you," one friend told me. "Just accept it." Of course, she was fifteen years older than I.

I tried to rationalize my distress at getting older. "Consider the alternative," I would tell myself. The only way not to grow old is to die young — and I sure didn't want to do that.

I clipped articles about people who did astounding things in the "prime of their life." (Whoever came up with that phrase?) For example:

- Cervantes was almost sixty when he began *Don Quixote.*
- Blind Fanny Crosby, writer of more than nine-thousand hymns, wrote her last hymn the day before she died at ninety-five.
- Corrie ten Boom's book, *The Hiding Place,* was published when she was seventy-eight.
- Thomas Hardy's greatest poetry was written when he was between the ages of seventy-five and eighty-five.
- Verdi was still composing music at eighty-five.
- Arthur Rubinstein gave a recital in Carnegie Hall at the age of eighty-nine, and Arturo Toscanini conducted various symphonies until close to his death at the age of ninety.
- Galileo, Edison, and Pavlov were still active in their seventies and eighties.
- At eighty-eight, Konrad Adenauer served as chancellor of West Germany, and at ninety-one, Eamon de Valera was president of Ireland.
- Clara Barton, founder of the Red Cross, was still working fourteen hours a day at the age of ninety.
- Marian Hart was eighty-four when she flew a single-engine airplane solo across the Atlantic.
- Ronald Reagan began the first of two terms as president just before he turned seventy.
- And, of course, the whole world knows of Grandma Moses who began painting at seventy-two and was still going strong at one-hundred.

But that was them, and this was me — getting older. And I didn't want to. Before I even reached fifty, AARP began sending me invitations to join. Then once I hit that half-century mark, friends began e-mailing me clever sayings pertaining to old age, such as:

The FREEDOM of *Letting Go*

OLD IS WHEN:
- Your friends compliment you on your new alligator shoes and you're barefoot.
- You are cautioned to slow down by your doctor instead of the police.

OR WITTY POEMS:

How do I know my youth is all spent?
Well, my get up and go has got up and went
But in spite of it all I am able to grin,
When I think of the places my get-up has been.

Old age is golden, so I've heard said,
But sometimes I wonder as I get into bed,
With my ears in the drawer, my teeth in a cup,
My eyes on the table until I wake up.
'Ere sleep dims my eyes, I say to myself,
"Is there anything else I should lay on the shelf?"

Since I have retired from life's competition,
I busy myself with complete repetition.
I get up each morning, dust off my wits,
Pick up the paper and read the obits.
If my name is still missing, I know I'm not dead,
So I eat a good breakfast and go back to bed.
—*Author Unknown*

I cut out wise sayings and taped them to the top of my computer monitor where I couldn't miss seeing them as I squinted to read the letters on the screen — letters that seemed to be getting smaller by the day. These sayings were supposed to be encouraging, like this one by Golda Meir:

> "Old age is like a plane flying through a storm. Once you're aboard, there's nothing you can do. You can't stop the plane, you can't stop the storm, and you can't stop time. So one might as well accept it calmly and wisely."

That's what bothered me. Most of the things in my life I had some control over: jobs, finances (somewhat), places we lived, my daily schedule. But there was *nothing* I could do about advancing age. I *couldn't* stop time. This enemy was totally out of my hands.

> *My uncle reads the obits every day. He can't understand how people always die in alphabetical order.*

I read in one place that the older you get, the more you should exercise. This makes you feel young? Then I saw the following exercise written by an unknown author and thought I might try it:

"For those of us getting along in years, here is a little secret for building your arm and shoulder muscles. Three days a week works well.

"Begin by standing straight with a five-pound potato sack in each hand. Extend your arms straight out from your sides and hold them there as long as you can. Try to reach a full minute and then relax. After a few weeks, move up to ten-pound potato sacks and then fifty-pound potato sacks.

"Eventually, try to get to where you can lift a hundred-pound potato sack in each hand and hold your arms horizontally, straight out from your sides, for more than a full minute. After you've reached a reasonable level of confidence at the hundred-pound sack level, start putting a couple of potatoes in each of the sacks, but be careful not to overdo it."[1]

Formal attire for retirees is tied shoes.

Author Lucy Neeley Adams says, "When I turned seventy-five, the various places that hurt quickly got my attention. However, the words of 2 Corinthians 4:7 bless me: 'We have this treasure in earthen vessels that the excellence of the power may be of God and not of [me].' The Treasure is what really matters. I have only a 'temporary temple.'"

She goes on to say, "One of our sons is named Scott. I have taken those letters from that verse –
S-acred
C-ontainer
O-f
T-he
T-treasure.
That helps me with my age burdens."

"*The ball doesn't know how old you are.*" (said of Tom Watson, fifty-nine-year-old winner of 2009 British Open golf tournament)

In his book, *Christian Maturity,* E. Stanley Jones shares how the biblical promise, "Even to your old age and gray hairs I ... will sustain you" (Isaiah 46:4 NIV) was fulfilled in his advanced years. When he passed seventy, God said to him, "I'm giving you the best years of your life — the next ten ahead." Jones added, "Two of them have passed and they have literally been the best two years of my life. Eight to go!...Practically all my question marks have now been straightened out into dancing exclamation points."[2]

Reading the above helped me realize that one of the secrets to aging gracefully was keeping busy. God's Word tells us that "The righteous shall flourish ... They will still bear fruit in old age." (Psalm 92:12,14)

The importance of being needed was brought out to me in dramatic fashion many years ago when I was a hospital patient. My elderly roommate was our landlord's mother-in-law. I overheard the doctor telling the daughter one day, "I can't find anything at all wrong with your mother. We'll have to release her." Then he asked, "Can you tell me what her days are like at home?"

"Oh," the daughter replied, "she lives with us. She has her own room and we don't let anyone bother her. She doesn't have to do any of the cooking or cleaning, and we don't ever let the children go into her room."

"That's what's wrong!" I heard the doctor say. "Let her help with the cooking and cleaning. Let the children ask her for help with their homework or play games with her. Let her come out of her bedroom and be a part of the family. Let her feel that she is still needed."

That wasn't my problem, however, I knew I was needed: by a husband who had taken a medical retirement at the age of forty-eight; by a daughter whose husband was in remission from MS; by another daughter with diabetes; by an elderly uncle living with us; and by a sister whose husband had a terminal illness. Yes, I was needed.

In years past, my writing — along with proofreading and editing for writers and publishers — had brought me satisfaction. But at this point in my life, it only brought discouragement. I didn't feel like beginning anything new because, after all, I was just going to die. So ... what did it matter? If I wrote something and it sold, I wouldn't even be around to see if what I wrote helped anyone. And it didn't make any difference how much money I made. It would just go to someone else.

Even completing a health questionnaire on the computer that showed I would live to be one-hundred and two didn't encourage me. How accurate could the test be? It showed that my husband — who was still kicking, in spite of all his health problems — died two years ago!

Years passed. Two granddaughters — one who insisted on calling me "Granny" — made me feel my age even more. Shopping for clothes and finding only those designed for Twiggy and Britney Spears didn't help any either.

Finally I began to pray about the problem that was taking such a hold on my life. I thanked the Lord for the health I had, for my family, for friends, and I asked him to give me a different perspective on "old age." It came from a totally unexpected source — the book of Haggai.

Our pastor, in a sermon on the rebuilding of the Temple, read from the second chapter of this Old Testament book. Verse 2 says, "Who is left among you that saw this house in her first glory?"

Her first glory. That sounds like me, I thought. My mind went back to what I believed were better days when I felt like doing more — days when I never missed calling on shut-ins or volunteering for jobs at church that needed doing. *Days when I was younger!* There it was again, that nagging thought. I couldn't stop getting older.

The pastor continued reading through the chapter, then he came to verse 9: "And the glory of this latter house shall be greater than that of the former!"

Greater than the former? Was it possible? The last part of my life could be more fruitful than the first? I don't think I heard any of the rest of the sermon. I only know the Lord revealed something to me that morning about my temple. I left church that day with those words running through my mind, and I actually woke up the next morning looking forward to the week ahead — something I hadn't done in a long time.

A few days later, I went to a nearby drugstore to buy some sugar substitute on sale. I couldn't find it so asked a young clerk for help. Then I moved over to the next aisle to pick up another item. A few minutes later, I heard the first clerk ask another salesperson, "Have you seen a little old gray-haired lady looking for some Sugar Twin?"

I walked over to them. "That's me," I said. "I'm your little old grey-haired lady." And I laughed! God had truly helped me to let go of my youth.

─♾ When I'm An Old Lady ♾─

When I'm an old lady, I'll live with each kid,
And bring so much happiness just as they did.
I want to pay back all the joy they've provided.
Returning each deed! Oh, they'll be so excited!
(When I'm an old lady and live with my kids)

I'll write on the wall with reds, whites and blues,
And I'll bounce on the furniture … wearing my shoes.
I'll drink from the carton and then leave it out.
I'll stuff all the toilets and oh, how they'll shout!
(When I'm an old lady and live with my kids)

The FREEDOM of *Letting Go*

When they're on the phone and just out of reach,
I'll get into things like sugar and bleach.
Oh, they'll snap their fingers and then shake their head,
And when that is done I'll hide under the bed.
(When I'm an old lady and live with my kids)

When they cook dinner and call me to eat,
I'll not eat my green beans or salad or meat,
I'll gag on my okra, spill milk on the table,
And when they get angry … I'll run … if I'm able!
(When I'm an old lady and live with my kids)

I'll sit close to the TV, through the channels I'll click,
I'll cross both eyes just to see if they stick.
I'll take off my socks and throw one away,
And play in the mud 'til the end of the day!
(When I'm an old lady and live with my kids)

And later in bed, I'll lay back and sigh,
I'll thank God in prayer and then close my eyes.
My kids will look down with a smile slowly creeping,
And say with a groan, "She's so sweet when she's sleeping!"
(When I'm an old lady and live with my kids)[3]

CHAPTER 9

LETTING GO OF GUILT

I was born with a guilt complex! It attached itself to my DNA in the delivery room, and continued to be my lifelong partner for years. While I dearly love the church I was brought up in — and am still a member of — I realized when I grew older how much its teachings helped feed this complex.

This was brought to light one day when my eight-year-old son told me, "Mom, except for the things you *don't* do, you're not much different than some of my friends' mothers. I thought Christians were supposed to have joy." Ouch! Somehow I had reached adulthood feeling you could be a Christian *or* have joy, but certainly not both. I felt guilty for almost everything I did.

I never had a problem accepting God's forgiveness for my sins, and I thank Him for it every day. But forgiving myself for things I'd done (or thought I'd done; for example, blaming myself for my dad leaving my mother when I was eleven years old. What did I do to cause him to leave?), that was another story. Up until recently, it seemed one thing or another nagged at me every day: words I said in anger, poor decisions I made, things I should have done but didn't — especially for two friends who were dying.

I was talking to a writer friend one day who was receiving chemo for terminal cancer. "Is there something special I can bring over?" I asked.

"I'd love some meat loaf," she said.

I laughed and replied, "Sorry, I'm not a meat loaf person, but I make good spaghetti!" She laughed too, switched to another subject and the conversation ended. She died later that week (and I didn't get the chance to take over spaghetti or meat loaf).

I told another friend undergoing kidney dialysis I would come over "someday" and play a game of Scrabble™ with her. But I put it off, not realizing how sick she really was, and she died before I followed through with my promise. I berated myself over and over for these two incidents. (This did help me in the days that followed, however, to not make promises to other friends who were in need physically or spiritually that I couldn't fulfill.)

Years ago, I felt especially guilty for a decision I pressured my husband to make that changed our entire future. When I confided in a preacher friend, he said, "When you don't forgive yourself, you crucify Christ again. You're saying He didn't really die for your sins so you keep reminding yourself of them every day." His advice helped then, but it didn't erase the problem altogether.

Guilt is a strange thing. Norman Vincent Peale says,

> "In dealing with guilt, the counselor often encounters the strange difficulty that, while an individual may feel that he has received the forgiveness of God, he is unable to forgive himself … There is a curious reluctance in the human mind to let go of guilt no matter how unpleasant. Strange indeed is the mind. It wants freedom and yet hesitates to take freedom when freely offered."[1]

When I was younger, all the evangelists who came to our church loved me because they knew at least one person would "come forward" every night. In fact, whenever I did something I felt was wrong, I could hardly wait until Sunday night so I could go to the altar and ask forgiveness.

I clearly remember one Monday night as a young teenager when I felt I had done something wrong. *I hate to wait until Sunday to go to the altar,* I thought, so I went upstairs to my room, knelt beside the bed, and told God I was sorry. Peace flooded over me — not just the peace of forgiveness, but the realization that I could ask for forgiveness anytime and anywhere and not have to carry the guilt all week.

False Guilt

Philip Yancey says, "We tend to think that our conscience is the voice of God, but it is really more the voice of our parents and our society, plus our experience, formed over many years." He refers to this as "false guilt" and says it "seldom stems from a specific action that can be changed."[2]

> *Guilt that comes from God is usually specific;*
> *from Satan, it is non-specific.*

I can definitely relate to this, as growing up, there were many things I was not allowed to do: wear makeup or jewelry, or go to movies or dances. (I had to get a note from our pastor and sit in the gym bleachers during the six weeks our P.E. class had dances.) My excuse to my friends was always, "My church doesn't believe in it." No reading Sunday newspapers, no eating out on Sundays (unless we stayed in town after the morning church service to attend an afternoon service at a little mission, then return to church at night). Even in the late '60s, when I taught a senior high Sunday school class, I couldn't take the teens bowling or to the local roller skating rink.

I didn't know how to differentiate between what was really wrong in God's sight or what were man-made laws, so to be safe, I asked forgiveness for everything I did. I didn't know there was a term for this until I was an adult and discovered it is called "legalism."

We can feel guilty because of things we have done — wrong or not. Often, it's because of things we haven't done. Neil Anderson says,

> "Legalists feel guilty for what they have said and done, or what they have not said and done. But when all is said and done, they've still not done enough. So they often feel like worthless failures, which leads to even more drivenness, and so on. Many driven performers find it nearly impossible to say 'no.' They are fearful that others will reject them if they refuse their requests … and rejection spells even more guilt and shame."[3]

Mary possessed many God-given talents, and she felt she should use all of them in her local church. A typical Sunday found her teaching a Sunday school class, then singing in the choir. In the evening she arrived an hour early to lead children's church, before singing in the choir in the evening service. Sometimes there were committee meetings between the services and even afterwards.

After working eight-hour days during the week, she often found herself back at church at night for choir practice, missionary meetings, and other obligations, with her mother babysitting her three young children. One night, as she was leaving, her five-year-old boy said, "Are you going away again tonight?"

And in the car, she sensed an inner voice say to her, "What good will it do to save other people's children if you lose your own?"

That week, she resigned all her positions except for her class and choir. However, this wasn't easy, as many in the church rebuked her for "not using the talents God gave her." False guilt!

A maxim she read during this time was a great help to her: "A need isn't necessarily a call."

A minister's wife found herself in a similar situation. The church's children's worship team was falling apart and, since she was on the Youth Steering Committee, she felt it was her responsibility to step in and help. Because she was also teaching the high school Sunday school class, and because she couldn't be in adult worship most of the time, she decided to stop singing in the choir.

"I still haven't heard the end of it," she says. "One woman — even after I explained my reasons — told me, 'Well, I just don't know if I could stand before my Lord, knowing I had not done all I could do.'

"Another woman, when she heard we had only a few children in children's worship, said, 'Ditch them. They're not worth it. You need to be in the choir. You have a gift and you need to use it.'

"I struggled with the guilt. It was tempting to cave in and think, 'If I just trusted the Lord, He would give me the strength to do it all!'"

In his book, *Codependency,* Pat Springle expands on this thought:

"Motivation by guilt is usually associated with the desire to avoid condemnation and the desire to perform, or measure up, to standards set by someone else or ourselves ... Our motivation is characterized by 'I have to' and 'I can't' statements:

- I have to accomplish this or that task today.
- I have to go here.
- I have to help this person in this way at this time.

- I have to say yes.
- I have to control my anger and hurt.
- I can't fail in this assignment.
- I can't let her down.
- I can't let my anger get out of control.
- I can't say no."[4]

Sources of Guilt

Guilt can come from many other sources. Unfortunately, as shown in Mary and the pastor's wife's stories, it too often can come from church leaders who find someone willing to accept a job (or someone who, because of guilt, can't say no) and overload them to the point of stress. Guilt can also come from preachers who dwell on the "shalt nots" of Christianity instead of inviting their congregation to revel in the joy and peace God provides when He forgives us of our sins.

Jesus Christ knows the things you've done wrong, but He did not come to rub them in, He came to rub them out. (Rick Warren)

Guilt can come from other Christians. I remember one dear "saint" whose favorite expression was, "I don't see how they can do that and call themselves Christian." (example: wearing toeless shoes).

A college friend prayed for several years for her mother. When she finally accepted Christ, a church member who was praying with her said, "Now that you're a Christian, you can't do thus-and-so any more." The mother never returned to church.

Guilt can also come from parents. "If you wouldn't have disobeyed me, you wouldn't have gotten hurt."

When we get older, guilt can come from our children. "You should have spent more time with me and raised me better. Then I wouldn't be having these problems today." (Like the hospital gave us an instruction manual when we brought our newborns home!) As one mother said, "Guilt — the gift that keeps on giving."

And, of course, much of our guilt comes from Satan. He comes as an "angel of light," telling us that the sins we have committed are too bad for God to forgive. A friend related a story to me about a woman in her church who had been a prostitute before she accepted Christ. Every time she prayed, however, there it was — her past. "God can't hear and answer your prayers," a voice said. But one day when she prayed, another Voice told her, "When I forgive a sin, it's gone. You are as cleansed and pure as if you had never committed that sin."

When Satan hurls the accusation at you that your past is too sinful to be forgiven, just remind him that God said, "As far as the east is from the west, so far has he removed our transgressions from us." (Psalm 103:12) As the old chorus puts it, He puts them "in the sea of [His] forgetfulness."

Corrie ten Boom says He then puts up a "No fishing" sign. She shares another beautiful example in her book, *Tramp for the Lord*:

"In Holland, there are many churches with belfries. The bells in the steeples are rung by hand with a rope that is pulled from the vestibule of the church. After the sexton lets go of the rope, the bell keeps on swinging. First *ding*, then *dong*. Slower and slower until there's a final *dong* and it stops. When sin is confessed and renounced, then Satan's hand is removed from the rope. But if we worry about our past bondage, Satan will use this opportunity to keep the echoes ringing in our minds …

Even though we sometimes have temptations, we are still free; Satan is no longer pulling the rope which controls our lives … Do not worry about the dings and dongs, they are nothing but echoes."[5]

Kitty Chappell, author of *I Can Forgive If I Want To — It's My Choice,* shared with me that when she speaks, she tells the listeners how she deals with recurring guilt:

"When Satan reminds me of a sin, I know it's him because God never reminds us of sins He's already forgiven. I say, 'Thank you, Satan, for reminding me of that sin. I'd forgotten how wonderful it was when God forgave me for it. Now I can praise Him again.' Satan is very unhappy when God is praised, so he stops reminding me. He knows God will be praised each time he does. I am never bothered with Satan's guilt."

Talk about freedom! Kitty's testimony reminds me of something our pastor said in a sermon:

"When I get to the Judgment and the book is opened, next to my name it will say, 'No sins' — not because I haven't committed any sins, but He has forgotten them, and He's the one who writes in the book. I'm the one who keeps picking up the pen.
"'Oh Lord, remember when I did this?'
"'No,' He says, 'I forgot. Put away the pen!'"

Peter

One of my favorite New Testament characters is Peter, probably because I feel there are more Peters in the church today than Pauls.

What a life Peter had! Called from his fishing nets to follow Christ, he was privileged to see Jesus heal the crippled and blind, and feed a multitude with five loaves of bread and two fish. This was the Messiah the world had long been waiting for. Thus, he was totally in shock and couldn't believe it when Jesus spoke of His upcoming death. After only three years, their Master was leaving them?

He was more in shock when Jesus said, "One of you will betray me." (Mark 14:18)

He's not talking about me, Peter said to himself smugly. Aloud he said, "Even if all fall away, I will not." (v. 29)

The third shock came when Jesus replied to him, " … before the rooster crows twice, you will deny me three times." (v. 30 NKJV)

You've got to be kidding! I'm one of Your inner circle. How could You say that about me? (Read the rest of the story in Mark 14:66-72, paraphrased below.)

Peter then watched as Jesus was arrested in the Garden of Gethsemane. And when the soldiers led Him away, Peter followed to see where they were going. A servant girl saw him and said, "I know you. You were with Jesus the Galilean."

"I don't know what you're talking about," Peter replied.

A second servant girl agreed. "This man was with Jesus of Nazareth."

Again Peter shook his head. "I don't know the man."

Then a third person said to him, "You're one of them. I can tell by the way you talk."

Peter began to curse and insisted, "I don't know the man."

Cock-a-doodle-doo!

Guilt! Can you even begin to imagine the guilt Peter felt? He had promised the Lord he would never betray Him, he would stand by Him no matter what. Now he had denied Him — not once, but three times!

And to make it worse, Jesus then turned and looked straight at him. Their eyes met. Peter would never forget that moment. So what did he do? He turned and ran.

Then came Sunday! The women went to the tomb and saw that the stone had been rolled away.

> "Entering the tomb, they saw a young man clothed in a long white robe sitting on the right side; and they were alarmed. But he said to them, 'Do not be alarmed. You seek Jesus of Nazareth, who was crucified. He is risen! He is not here. See the place where they laid Him. But go, tell His disciples — and Peter — that He is going before you into Galilee; there you will see Him, as He said to you." (Mark 16:6-7 NKJV)

Tell His disciples — and Peter! Tell him that he is forgiven. Tell him he doesn't have to carry his load of guilt any more.

GUILT IN LATER YEARS

If you've struggled with guilt most of your life, you may find that the problem increases as you grow older. This can also impact your spiritual life. Norman Vincent Peale says that:

> "In youth and even in the strong middle years, [guilt's] effects may be in part at least halted, but with the declining vitality of advancing years and the heavier burden of responsibilities which comes with maturity, resistance declines and the long held infection of guilt rushes out to dominate the entire system."[6]

I found this to be true in my own life. Because I was the youngest of four children, and born with a birth defect that required me to wear a brace on my arm for several years, I had a deep sense of low self-esteem. When my father left, not knowing the reason behind his going, I wondered what *I* had done to make him leave.

Because I began work at a young age to help bring needed money into the house, I was somewhat of a loner throughout my high school years. Upon graduation, I received a scholarship and was able to attend a nearby college.

I wasn't sure what I wanted to do with my life, until one morning I read the Scripture verse, "I will give thee the heathen for thine inheritance" (Psalm 2:8 KJV), and decided I was called to be a missionary. I spoke of my call at a number of missionary rallies. Before my second year of college, a friend talked me into quitting college and entering nurses' training, telling me I could help "heal bodies as well as souls."

My church gave me a sendoff party, including gifts such as white shoes and hosiery, a nurse's watch, and other needed supplies. At the end of three months, however, I knew nursing wasn't for me and I returned home — full of guilt and ashamed to face my church friends.

At the age of twenty, I moved seven-hundred and fifty miles away from home for a dream job. In this new city, I met my future husband — a seminary student, and later he accepted a small church. Here again, however, guilt reared its ugly face, as he ended up resigning the church after one year because of my health.

Because of all the guilt I faced during those years, as I got older, I began to doubt many of the basic Christian principles I had accepted by faith all my life. *Is there really a heaven? And if there is, with all the things I've done, will I make it? Forgive myself? Impossible!*

In his book, *Making Your Emotions Work for You,* Harold J. Sala asks the question, "If you understand that God has forgiven you, what right do you think you have not to forgive yourself? Are you greater than He?"

He goes on to say, "Your failing to forgive yourself robs you of peace of mind ... It is a burden that God doesn't want you to bear, and in a very real sense it renders what Christ did of no effect because you bear the guilt of your failure, one that He bore long ago."

Sala asks us to picture Jesus as He hung on the cross. At the time, the Romans would write on a piece of parchment the crime for which the person was executed and place it on the cross for all to see. "Now," Sala says, "think about the ... sin or deed that troubles you, as if it were written on a piece of parchment and affixed to the cross as the crime for which Jesus died. Picture the blood that flowed from His wounds covering that writing until it is obliterated forever."[7]

The above illustration was graphically brought home to me recently and helped silence my guilt once and for all. While going through a stressful period in our family, thoughts kept nagging me: I should have been a better mother. I shouldn't have wasted so much money through the years. I shouldn't have quit the jobs I did. (One was forty-eight years ago!) I shouldn't have said what I did to my husband (many times). The guilt weighed me down.

Then, one Sunday while singing a familiar song in church — one I've sung all my life and know by heart — the words took on a new meaning and brought tears to my eyes:

"My sin — oh, the bliss of this glorious tho't!
My sin — *not in part, but the whole* —
Is nailed to the cross and I bear it no more.
Praise the Lord, praise the Lord, O my soul!"[8]

Suddenly it hit me: *All* of my sin — committed, as well as mistakes that in my guilt I felt were sin — was nailed to the cross. Decisions I'd made in haste, words I'd said, things I had or hadn't done — they were *all* nailed to the cross. And if that was true — and it is — why was I still bearing the burden that Christ took upon Himself?

"Sin walks us into a huge warehouse filled with video clips of our life and says, 'This is your life. We have thousands of clips of your failures. Many of them are so embarrassing that you wouldn't want to show them to your children. That is all you are, and we have the record of it. So you might as well surrender to sin within, because you can't be better than this. You are these clips, and nothing else.'

"Well, [the good news is] Jesus has burned the warehouse!"[9]

*****

And that, my friend, is freedom!

CHAPTER 10

LETTING GO OF CONTROL

I never felt that I was a controlling person or one who liked to be in control; however, an incident happened a few years ago that caused me to think differently. I was visiting my home state and, not wanting to rent a car, I depended on others to drive me around. One day, I waited for a relative to pick me up and take me to another town to have lunch with other family members. I waited … and waited … and waited. At the time we were to meet the others — an hour away — my ride showed up. (In her defense, she did have a good reason for being late.) It was then that I realized I didn't necessarily want to always be in control but, at the same time, I didn't like it when *someone else* was in control.

> "At any given moment, thousands, maybe even millions, of Americans feel they've lost control — over jobs, spouses, kids, health, time. The problem is driving people into doctors' offices with psychological and medical diseases, at untold human and economic cost. (Up to ninety percent of all visits to doctors are for stress-related ailments.) The urge to take control, or at least feel in control, has never been greater."[1]

Writer Dean Nelson tells about the time he was refereeing a men's touch football game. A fight broke out, which he tried to break up, but before he could separate the combatants, he was grabbed by the back of the shirt and flung aside like a limp towel. He writes, "As I picked myself up off the ground, I was struck with this question: Who's in charge here? The fight ended, and the game went on, but I still wasn't sure who was in charge. I knew it wasn't me."

Nelson went on to say, "Sometimes we find ourselves asking the same question, yet God was, is and always will be on His throne ... Circumstances may make it seem that the world is out of control, but ... just think — the God who rules the universe still gives us the choice of whether we also want Him to rule our minds and hearts."[2]

Who's the Boss?

I once babysat two sisters — the youngest a very independent three-year-old. She not only cried every day when her mother left her at my house, but she refused to mind — no matter what. I talked to her mother one day, who was a good friend of mine. "You just have to show her who's boss," she replied.

So, the next day when "Julie" disobeyed, I asked her, "Who's the boss here?"

"I am," she stated defiantly, upon which I sent her to the bedroom.

Twice more she came out, and when I asked her the same question, I received the same answer.

Then I felt a gentle tap on my shoulder. Turning around, I repeated, "Who's the boss?"

"You are," she said.

The next morning, when the mother pulled up in our driveway, Julie threw open the car door and ran to meet me, throwing her arms around my neck.

"What happened?" the mother asked. "When she got up this morning, she could hardly wait to get here."

"We just agreed on who was the boss," I replied with a smile.

No matter the situation, one person must be in charge, and the others have to submit to that authority. And in the Christian life, God must be in control.

Our pastor asked the following question in his sermon one Sunday, "What happens when we are in charge?" and then he gave the following answers:

1. We follow our own desires instead of God's.
2. We have a false sense of security.
3. We lose our sense of peace, but then something comes to shake us up.
4. Other people suffer because of our disobedience.
5. We pay the price of disobedience.

He said, "People have been Christians for thirty to forty years and are riding a spiritual roller coaster — up and down — because they haven't settled the control issue. When God has control," he went on, "the Holy Spirit is the Comforter, but when you have control, the Holy Spirit is the Convictor."

Today I had a battle,
The fight was hard and long;
My opponent was so stubborn,
And I knew him to be wrong.
We didn't need a referee,
Because, when we were through,
The decision was unquestioned,
Nor did we start anew.

I never did like fighting,
And yet I fail to see
How I could help but cheer a bit
When I had conquered ME! — Hazel V. Wolfe

In her book, *Out of Control and Loving It,* Lisa Bevere explains how those who control their lives, relationships, and surroundings are actually in bondage. The freedom they seek is lost. "Conversely, those who have relinquished control to the Lord are the ones who are actually in control and walk in life and freedom."[3]

A pastor's wife wrote, "I have always rejoiced in God's will when it coincided with what I wanted, but … deep in my heart, I wanted to be the boss. I wanted to make my own plans for my life. I wanted to snatch my life back from the gentle hands of God and hold it to my chest, growling, 'I've changed my mind. I don't really like what You've planned for me.' The problem is," she added, "when you give your life to Christ, He takes it. You can't just loan it to Him … Giving God control of my life became much easier once I realized He already had it."[4]

Have you ever been in a hospital with rails all around your bed and hooked up to IVs? You couldn't get up without help, and you felt totally out of control? A friend wrote me a few years ago of her experience preceding the birth of her daughter.

"I was shocked when my blood pressure started going crazy, and I was hospitalized and then had delivery induced. I hated the vulnerability and lack of control of the hospital, and truthfully, I was surprised to discover how scared I was even being in the hospital, which I never expected. Most of all, I hated being 'out of control.' Of course, God availed Himself of the opportunity to show me He was in control, not me."

The FREEDOM of *Letting Go*

CONTROLLING OTHERS

It used to be when I was upset with my husband over something, he'd say, "What's wrong?"

I'd reply, "Nothing!" (thinking, *He should know. He did it!*) Then I'd give him the silent treatment, and begin to furiously clean house — noisily slamming doors and drawers.

One day after one of our "discussions," I sensed the Lord saying to me, "I thought we took care of this 'letting go' thing."

"Oh, we did, Lord," I answered. "I've let go of many things that happened to me in the past." He then reminded me that "ten minutes ago is in the past." After that, when something bothered me, I let my husband know right away. We talked it out, and then I let it go. It was simply a matter of wanting to be in control of a situation. (Of course, now my house isn't as clean!)

Instead of attempting to control what I can't,
perhaps I can learn to let go of my plans and say, "Thank You, God,
for choosing this season for me." (Cecil Murphey)

My friend, Cindy Scinto, shares the following in her book, *A Heart Like Mine*:

"My husband [John] barely seventeen when I latched onto him, became the object of my desire to gain control and comfort. I looked to him to fulfill my shortcomings — the areas where I had no reins to steer and direct.

"We married six years after John asked me to go steady. Our relationship appeared to be the perfect courtship. Even the circumstances for his proposal were cleverly manipulated by my need to move out from the clutches of my home life. I became the decision maker and controller. I did not allow my husband to take his place as spiritual leader and head of our household. Overwhelmed by my dominating design, he became reclusive, leaving me to deal with all the matters of our marriage. It made for an unbalanced and insecure relationship.

"When our son came along and financial and medical problems mounted, I demanded that John step in and fix everything. But I had created a lopsided relationship that needed drastic measures to be righted. With much heartbreak, we sought the help of a Christian counselor. After several sessions, this gentle, gracious counselor looked at me and said, 'You have to let go of your desire to control everything. Let your husband be who he needs to be in this marriage.' I instantly was deflated. Had I really taken control? Hadn't I given up the 'old me' a long time ago when I asked Jesus to be my Lord? No, there was much more to the cleansing than I ever could foresee. This was merely a small advance to be rid of a deep-rooted cause."[5]

Later in the book, Cindy shares the night she came to the end of herself:

" ... the tears began and I sobbed the innermost nuggets of pain from my broken heart. All the issues from my past — that is, my Christian past, of which I took control and rid myself — were being paraded in front of me one by one. The Lord grabbed each circumstance and held it up to my face, letting me know there was trash onto which I was holding tightly. For the first time, I clearly could see my problem with control. I sought to control my life, my spiritual state, my circumstances, my purpose and even my destiny.

The FREEDOM of *Letting Go*

"For someone who thought she had let go of all control, I now realized I was safely hiding the last fragments of my own domination.

"What I did with many issues throughout the years was to conquer them on my own and neatly tuck them away. The problem with such annihilation is that a complete ridding of bitterness, scars, anger, sin, unforgiveness and other roots of hurt cannot happen unless the Lord gets complete control …

"I paid attention to the deep sermons on letting go and I profusely studied how to grow close to the Lord to let Him control my life. When I confidently awarded myself with an A+ for passing the school of letting go, He stripped me down to bare my soul and exposed my folly."[6]

Too often, our motto is like that of Frank Sinatra, who sang, "I did it my way." I couldn't help but think how appropriate those words were when sung at the funeral of one of my employers. A successful businessman who was used to being in control of people, of situations, and especially of his own body, he had finally grown tired of his constant struggle with an incurable disease and took his own life.

Controlling the Tongue

I have a friend who can speak in front of hundreds of people without a bit of fear, but she was very self-conscious when in a small group. She covered up her low self-esteem with nervous chatter, often interrupting others to share something that happened to her, or to one-up someone else's story. Although she was vaguely aware of this personality trait, she did not realize how irritating it was to others until a dear friend took her aside and, in love, prayed with her about it.

Evangelist Michael B. Ross says, "People who are not at rest with themselves or with God find it difficult to control their tongues. There is nothing morally wrong with monopolizing a conversation at a party. The issue of the uncontrolled tongue is not how much we talk, but whether we can be silent when it would be better not to speak."[7]

Some people, when there's even the tiniest bit of silence, think they should fill it with their wisdom.

Monopolizing a conversation is, in itself, a form of controlling a situation in which you feel out of control. If this is your problem, it might help you to realize that you are a thief: You are stealing other people's time, stealing their chances to share a story, a bit of wisdom or perhaps a prayer request. Someone has said that there's a reason God gave us only one mouth but two ears. He wanted us to listen twice as much as we talk.

To determine if you are a good listener, ask yourself the following questions:

1. Do I allow the speaker to finish without interrupting?
2. Do I listen "between the lines?" (Someone referred to this as "listening with the third ear." What the person says may not have anything to do with what they are feeling inside.)
3. Do I tune out distractions when listening?
4. Do I make an effort to seem interested in what the other person is saying?

One girl said about her mother, "She needs to talk a lot because it gives her control of conversations." When God has control of your life, you will no longer feel the need, as did this mother, to control others through excessive chatter.

The FREEDOM of *Letting Go*

> *"I will take heed to my ways, that I sin not with my tongue;*
> *I will keep my mouth with a bridle."* (Psalm 39:1 KJV)

CONTROL OVER SITUATIONS

A number of years ago, my nephew, Dave Clark, traveled with a Southern gospel singing group. During this time, the daughter of the group's leader became very ill. One day the father said, "It just seems like I ought to be able to do *something*. I feel so helpless." From this situation, my nephew wrote the following song:

Brokenhearted people, I see them ev'ry day,
And I wish that I could be the one to take their hurt away;
But all my good intentions can't take away the need,
But I found a friend in Someone Who is all I cannot be.

People all around me, They see the way I live,
At times it seems they're reaching out for love that I can't give;
And all that I can hope for is that somehow they will see
A love that comes from Someone Who is all I cannot be.

Jesus is all the things that I can never be,
He is ever watching over me, and He knows just what I need;
When I've fallen short of ev'rything the world expects of me,
I've found a Friend in Someone Who is all I cannot be.[8]

So many situations are out of our control. In my small writers' critique group, one member's mother-in-law just died of a brain tumor; another member's father-in-law and mother-in-law recently died; her son-in-law just returned to work after a two-year illness and her husband is in relapse from cancer; another member and her husband both lost their jobs several months ago; one member lost her husband two years ago; one's daughter and son-in-law went through several years of infertility before adopting a newborn baby; our oldest member's life was turned upside down when she was hit by a pickup truck; another woman's husband was just diagnosed with Alzheimer's, and my own husband and daughter have health problems.

> *Let us then take comfort in this fact: When things are out of our control, Jesus has it all in His control.* (John McLaughlin)

In most of these cases, there is nothing we can do in our own strength. We worry and fret, we agonize over what to do — when in some cases there is *nothing* we can do, and we lose sleep — all because we *want* to somehow control the situation. God urges us to cease our striving. His Word tells us that, "He will not let you stumble and fall; the one who watches over you will not sleep. Indeed, he who watches over Israel never tires and never sleeps." (Psalm 121:3-4 NLT)

And if *He* never sleeps, why should both of us stay awake?

Elisabeth Elliott shares the story of Amy Carmichael in her first year of missionary work in Japan. She and a missionary couple were held up on a journey because of a boat that did not arrive. Not just hours, but days, went by, and the young missionary began to fret because of the time lost and the consequences to others who counted on them. The older missionary said calmly, "God knows all about the boats." This became a maxim of faith for Carmichael for the rest of her life.[9]

A year after my night of letting go in Michigan, I traveled out of state for a conference, arriving at the airport gate at 5 p.m. No one was

The FREEDOM of *Letting Go*

there to meet me. I ate a bite, worked some puzzles, edited some manuscripts and tried to think of all the things to be thankful for — you know, "in everything give thanks." Finally, at 10:10 p.m., someone picked me up. (Turned out the instructions I received were missing one sheet, which told me — and two others — where to meet.)

The next day another staff member said to me, "I can't believe you weren't more upset over what happened last night."

"A year ago, I would have been," I told her, sharing with her my "letting go" experiences. "This past year my motto has been 'God's in control,' and I have to believe He's in control of the little things as well as the big."

"Then you've learned the real secret of letting go," she said. "You've learned to *let go of control.*"

CHAPTER 11

LETTING GO OF WORRY

My husband is a professional worrier. Since, like most men, he worries about finances, I often tell him I'm going to hire him out to our friends. They can give him a list of their problems and walk away, carefree, knowing he'll worry for them.

One day he was listing all the family members he was concerned about. Then he added, "And I'm worried about the country and where it's headed."

"It's a good thing God has you to help Him," I said. "He'd never make it without you."

"Yep!" he grinned. "I'm His assistant."

I then shared with him a saying by Stephenie Geist, "If worrying was an Olympic sport, you'd get the gold for sure."

For peace of mind, resign as general manager of the universe.

Dr. James Fowler says,

"To worry is to assume a responsibility that is not necessarily ours to assume; failing to recognize that God is bigger than any problem we might have, and loves us enough to seek our highest good in the midst of every situation … Worry is a form of humanistic self-orientation that thinks, 'It's up to me to take care of this situation,' and is thus a form of practical atheism, acting as if there is no God to deal with the situation, or that God doesn't know or care about the situation."[1]

Our pastor told our congregation one Sunday, "Worry is what I do best. If I worry hard enough, I can find a solution to my problem. I can figure this out. I can solve this. The focus is on *I* instead of *God*." He added, "Faith is not just trusting God and doing nothing, but doing what you can do, all you can do, then trusting God for the results. Do your best, give God the rest."

Then he shared this story. Their car was clean, windows washed, everything in shape for a family trip. A few miles down the road, a bug lit on the windshield. He made the mistake of turning on the wipers and — you can guess what happened — it only made the problem worse. "Worry is like turning on the wipers," he said. "It makes a little speck bigger."

This is similar to what David said in Psalm 94:19, "My anxious thoughts multiply within me."

In Googling the word "worry," I was amazed to learn that there actually is such a thing as a "worry doll."

"Dolls that remove worries — or trouble dolls — are very small and colorful dolls traditionally made in Guatemala. A person (usually a child) who cannot sleep due to worrying can express their worries to a doll and place it under their pillow before going to sleep. Some medical centers use them in conjunction with treatment for disease in children. According to folklore, the doll is thought to worry in the person's place, thereby permitting the person to sleep peacefully. The person will wake up without their worries, which have been taken away by the doll during the night. Parents may remove the doll during the night, reinforcing the child's belief that the worry is gone."[2]

There are also "worry beads" — known as *komboloi* — that resemble prayer beads but, unlike them, bear no religious significance. They are merely an instrument of relaxation and stress management. A more modern version of worry beads are called "wigglers," and users claim that wiggling these beads creates a rush of adrenaline, followed by a soothing, calm sensation.[3]

The University of Idaho Counseling & Testing Center suggests that people schedule a time for worrying. When a worry comes to mind, tell yourself you will worry about it at a specific time (say 6 p.m.). Then, when 6 p.m. arrives, you take fifteen or twenty minutes to examine your worries of the day.[4]

What would happen if, instead of taking that fifteen or twenty minutes to worry, we use that time to pray, or go to a concordance and find verses that challenge our worrying tendencies?

> "Do not fret ... trust in the LORD ... Commit your way to the LORD ... be still before the LORD." (Psalm 37:1, 3, 5, 7)

> "Cast your cares on the LORD and he will sustain you." (Psalm 55:22)

> Then Jesus said to his disciples: " ... do not worry about your life, what you will eat; or about your body, what you will wear. Life is more than food, and the body more than clothes. Consider the ravens: They do not sow or reap, they have no storeroom or barn; yet God feeds them. And how much more valuable you are than birds! Who of you by worrying can add

a single hour to his life? Since you cannot do this very little thing, why do you worry about the rest?" (Luke 12:22-26)

"Be careful, or your heart will be weighed down with ... the anxieties of life." (Luke 21:34)

"Do not be anxious about anything, but in everything, by prayer and petition, with thanksgiving, present your requests to God. And the peace of God ... will guard your hearts and your minds in Christ Jesus." (Philippians 4:6-7)

"The Lord is my helper; I will not be afraid. What can man do to me?" (Hebrews 13:6)

"Cast all your anxiety on Him because He cares for you." (1 Peter 5:7)

When we moved to Arizona for my husband's health, it took six months for him to find a job he was physically able to do. With three small children, bills piled up. One morning, during my quiet time, I felt compelled to read one of my favorite promises found in Philippians 4:19, as I needed to be reminded that God would supply our needs.

I read it, and then read it again. *Surely it must be a typo,* I thought. But no, this verse in the King James Version reads, "My God shall supply all your *need* according to his riches in glory by Christ Jesus." God reminded me, "You have only one need, and that is to stay close to Me, then I will supply all your other needs."

Said the robin to the sparrow,
"I would really like to know
Why those anxious human beings
Rush about and worry so."
Said the sparrow to the robin,
"Well, I think that it must be
That they have no heavenly Father
Such as cares for you and me."[5]

Worrying About the Past

Some people spend much of their time worrying over the past — decisions they made, things they can't undo. John Newton, author of the beloved hymn, "Amazing Grace," said, "We can easily manage if we will only take, each day, the burden appointed to it. But the load will be too heavy for us if we carry yesterday's burden over again today, and then add the burden of the morrow before we are required to bear it."[6]

When I finally accepted my mother's passing, a friend who had known me for years said, "You seem different somehow."

"I *am* different," I told her. Not only had I let go of my mother, but I had learned the whole *principle* of letting go of *many* things. "It takes a lot of energy to carry the past around with you," I explained. "When you let go of it, you have more energy for other things."

Proverbs 12:25 tells us, "Anxiety in the heart of man weighs it down."

It's as Rev. David Roth, a Colorado pastor, says,

"Another way to think of the futility of worry is to imagine someone carrying around a suitcase of old junk that he doesn't use. If he complained to you about his aching back, wouldn't you suggest he drop the suitcase?

"But we tend to do the same thing, feeling troubled, tired and pulled off-balance. We hang on to our burden because (we think) something bad might happen if we let it go. But the answer is so easy. If we simply let go — if we trust in the Lord — we suddenly feel lighter."[7]

You can clutch the past so tightly to your chest that it leaves your arms too full to embrace the present. (Jan Glidewell)

WORRY OVER THE FUTURE

An old song titled "I Don't Know About Tomorrow" includes the following words in its chorus:

Many things about tomorrow,
I don't seem to understand;
But I know who holds tomorrow,
And I know who holds my hand.[8]

I remember a white-haired Scottish lady singing the first two lines this way:

Many things about tomorrow,
I don't need to understand.

How right she was! When we know who holds tomorrow and we know who holds our hand, we don't have to worry over the future. The first and third verses of this song also give us assurance:

I don't know about tomorrow,
I just live from day to day.
I don't borrow from its sunshine,
For its skies may turn to gray.
I don't worry o'er the future,
For I know what Jesus said,
And today I'll walk beside Him,
For He knows what is ahead …

I don't know about tomorrow,
It may bring me poverty;
But the one who feeds the sparrow,
Is the one who stands by me.
And the path that be my portion,
May be through the flame or flood,
But His presence goes before me,
And I'm covered with His blood.

What Do We Worry About?

Unemployment. At the time of this writing, the national unemployment rate stood at 8.8 percent, with some states as high as 14 percent. When McDonald's recently announced they were hiring fifty-thousand new employees, among the applicants were teachers and truck drivers who had lost their jobs.

It's hard not to worry when you're out of work and fear losing your home, but God knows where you are and He will not abandon you. The words of a song recorded by Karen Wheaton and others, "He'll Do It Again," remind us that He's always come through for us, and He's the same now as then.

The FREEDOM of *Letting Go*

In my late teens, I was looking for work when a friend called and offered me a job at The Apothecary Shop — a local pharmacy. The position paid $1.00 an hour (a good rate back then); however, it meant I would have to work Sundays and sell liquor "for medicinal purposes." I prayed about it, and my mother said, "If in doubt, leave it out." I turned it down.

The next week I applied at a new grocery store, which also had a liquor department. However, I was offered a job at an existing store in the chain. Because that store was near a school, it was not allowed to sell liquor. The pay — $1.49 an hour!

A pastor's wife who started work with me the same day said, "Do you know that out of four-hundred who applied at the new store, you and I were the only two hired for this store?" She added, "I was offered another job this week, but turned it town because I would have to work Sundays and sell liquor."

"Where was that?" I asked, unbelieving.

"At The Apothecary Shop," she replied.

Before we moved to Arizona, our friends warned us that the job situation was not good, yet my husband thought with his years of grocery store experience, he wouldn't have any problem finding something.

The day we arrived, we stopped to visit a friend and, while there, my husband called a nearby grocery store. He was told, "The supervisor who does the hiring won't be in until tomorrow, but you can come in and fill out an application."

We drove to the store, the supervisor just happened to drop in that afternoon, and my husband was hired on the spot!

The next day I found a job at a local newspaper office; however, my job was in one town, my husband's in another, and we were staying with a friend in a third location. Because our work schedules varied and we had only one car, I soon gave notice at my job so I could look for a place to live.

After we found our own place, I saw an ad in the paper that the State of Arizona was going to hold an "Operation Hire" on the next Saturday. Personnel from all the state departments would be on hand to interview prospective employees. I decided to go.

The first interview they sent me on was at the Highway Department, keeping track of materials inventory. "If you don't like it, we have another temporary job you might be interested in," the woman at Operation Hire said before giving me the location.

The job sounded boring and was quite a distance from our house, so I decided to apply at the temporary job, which was at the State House of Representatives.

"Do you take shorthand?" the steno pool supervisor asked. I shook my head. "Well, go ahead and fill out an application anyway," she said.

I filled it out, and halfway up to her desk to return it, I remembered I had used a word processor in my previous job — a new machine called an MTST (Magnetic Tape Selectric Typewriter). Even though I had used it for only two weeks, I decided to add it to my application.

I had just returned home when the phone rang. "I see you used an MTST," the supervisor said. "We could use someone to fill in when some of the other secretaries are busy."

I returned to the Capitol on Monday and was hired. (I never did use the MTST that session.)

Daily Needs. At the beginning of our second winter in Arizona, my husband was working two part-time jobs, yet money was still scarce. I had gone through our children's clothes, determining what they needed for cold weather. (Yes, it does get cold in Arizona!) I knelt and prayed, "Lord, Bob's okay, but Janet and Patty really need long pants."

I was still on my knees when the phone rang. A woman from our church who had three daughters was on the line. "I've been going through our girls' things and they have a bunch of long pants they've outgrown. Can you use them?"

I shouldn't have been surprised, for doesn't God's Word assure us, "Before they call I will answer; while they are still speaking I will hear," (Isaiah 65:24) and, "Do not worry … what you shall wear … your heavenly Father knows that you need them" (Matthew 6:25, 34)?

Moving to a New Location. It's hard to let go of familiar places. Some people never do. They continue to live in the past, remembering how it was "where we used to live." For a long time after moving to Arizona, I continued to take my hometown paper. I compared everything in our new state to how it was "at home" — weather, prices, schools, churches. It took almost twenty-four years for me to let go.

While thinking about how hard it was for me to move to a new place, I thought of women in the Bible — for example, Mary, the mother of Jesus. I'm sure she didn't plan on spending the first Christmas day in Bethlehem. In preparing for her baby's birth, she probably had a midwife lined up and looked forward to showing off her new son to family members and friends who lived in Nazareth. But she and Joseph needed to be in Bethlehem to fulfill the prophecy spoken by the prophet Micah: "But you, Bethlehem … out of you will come for me one who will be ruler over Israel … " (5:2)

That wasn't Mary's last move. I have a special attachment to the place where our children were born, so I can imagine Mary's feeling when Joseph woke her up one night. "Get packed," he told her. "We're moving to Egypt."

"Egypt! Why Egypt?"

"Well, an angel told me in a dream to go to Egypt."

It would have been easy for Mary to complain, "Jesus was born here. We have friends here. It's too difficult to travel such a long distance with a baby. It's too far from our families."

Or Joseph might have said to the angel, "I have work here. I've built up a good carpentry business."

But he didn't resist, nor did Mary. They were obedient to God's messengers and, in so doing, they helped save Baby Jesus from Herod's slaughter.

Then there is the story of Naomi in the Old Testament, who had not only lost her husband, but both her sons as well. She told her two daughters-in-law — Ruth and Orpah — "I'm going back to where I used to live. You two can return to your families where you used to live."

Orpah left, but Ruth insisted on going with Naomi. "Don't urge me to leave you or to turn back from you," she said. "Where you go I will go, and where you stay I will stay. Your people will be my people and your God my God." (Ruth 1:16-17)

It must have been difficult for Ruth to move to a new country where she knew no one; however, she didn't complain. God rewarded her loyalty by giving her Boaz as a husband and allowing her to be an ancestor of the Messiah.

Then there was Abraham who "by faith ... went, even though he did not know where he was going." (Hebrews 11:8)

The FREEDOM of *Letting Go*

Housing. The apostle Paul said he had learned to be content in whatever state he was. I know he wasn't referring to location, but it took me awhile to be content in my new state. It was hard leaving my family, friends, and home church in Michigan, but my husband's health could no longer take the cold climate. We thought finding jobs would be the hardest challenge we would face, but it turned out that finding a house was even more difficult.

We moved to Arizona in early December and hoped to be in our own home before Christmas. Our three children — seven, six, and four years old — just hoped we would have a Christmas tree to put the presents under.

For three weeks we scoured the want ads, and even drove up and down streets, knocking at neighbors' doors whenever we saw an empty house. One day, after looking at a four-bedroom, unfurnished house that cost four times the rent in our hometown, we returned to our friend's home just as the telephone rang.

"Our daughter is moving out-of-state," a voice said. "Would you like to look at her house?"

Would we? Not only was it in the city where we wanted to live, furnished (including a piano), and one-third the rent of the four-bedroom house, we also ended up getting four days free rent. And the pièce de résistance: In answer to our children's prayers, the former residents left a Christmas tree in the living room, all decorated!

What People Think About You. Phil McGraw's dad told him, "You wouldn't worry so much about what people thought about you if you knew how seldom they did."

Many of our decisions are based on our fear of what others will think. A good friend shared the following story:

"The problem began with my unwed daughter's pregnancy. I did not want her to keep the baby, but I was the only one. I was so afraid of what others would say about this bi-racial infant.

"The baby boy left the hospital at two days old to stay for fifteen days with the foster mother, while his mother (no, his *grandmother*) made up her mind about what to do with him. We had three more days before he would be gone for good to adoptive parents (who didn't yet know they were to get the baby, thank goodness).

"One quiet morning, sitting alone while my husband and daughter slept, I opened my Bible and a passage from 1 Corinthians 1:20 leaped out at me. 'Where is the wise?...Hath not God made foolish the wisdom of this world?' (KJV) I knew that was for ME!

"My shame, anger, unforgiveness and fear of what others would say — and every negative thing that had flooded my mind for the past nine months — I now knew was not God's wisdom. My wisdom was too pitiful for words. Crying, I surrendered to His ways.

"Today, that gorgeous grandson is nineteen. We would *not* want to do without him for the world. He is dearly loved and cherished, and we praise God every day for giving him to us. All my worry was for naught."

Making Decisions. Some people waste their time worrying about things that are out of their control, such as children who are gone from the home, the national debt, the weather. (One friend worries constantly because her home is located near an earthquake fault.)

There is no use worrying about things over which you have no control, and if you have control, you can do something about them instead of worrying. (S.C. Allyn)

The FREEDOM of *Letting Go*

However, others worry about things that are in their control, such as decisions that must be made. They agonize over which path to choose, and after they finally make their decision, they second-guess themselves and wonder, *Should I have chosen the other path?*

"Cease striving and know that I am God," the Word says in Psalm 46:10. (NASB)

Our pastor said one Sunday, "You don't have to have all the answers and everything spelled out, but you can have clarity. God will always show you the next step. You don't need to know more than that."

One difficult decision for many is finding God's will for their life — whether in a choice of college, a move to a new location or to know if God is calling you to work in a particular field. I mentioned earlier my discouragement and disillusionment after dropping out of nurses' training. I was confused as to God's will for my future. A letter from a close friend suggested that I consider the following points:

1. Write down the talents God has given you.
2. Give yourself enough time to be sure.
3. Ask yourself if the call increases or decreases as time goes on.
4. Be sure you're listening to God, not someone else.
5. Be *fully* surrendered — give God your *all*.
6. Don't let anything or anyone stand in your way, and finally,
7. Be *completely* honest with God and yourself.

Praying over the above advice helped me reach a decision — one that didn't involve nursing or missions, but, rather, another field where I could use my God-given gifts. Dale Carnegie says, in making a decision:

1. Get the facts.
2. Analyze the facts.
3. Arrive at a decision, and then act on that decision.⁹

That works for me. First, I write out the problem at the top of the page. Often, just putting it in writing clarifies it for me and I can make a decision without going further. But, if I need more help, I make two columns — one "for" and one "against" what I want to do. At the end, one side usually outweighs the other, and using those factors — along with prayer, Scripture, and advice from godly counselors — I can make my decision.

A girl in her early twenties who was dating two young men (neither of which her parents approved of) used this method to see which person she should continue seeing. At the end of the two lists, she threw down her pen and said (to her mother's delight), "I don't want either of them." (She's now a minister's wife.)

One of my favorite songs is the old hymn, "Lead, Kindly Light" — especially the last two lines of verse 1:

Keep Thou my feet; I do not ask to see
The distant scene; one step enough for me.¹⁰

Worry Causes Disease

According to WebMD,

"[Worry can cause]: difficulty swallowing, dizziness, dry mouth, fast heartbeat, fatigue, headaches, inability to concentrate, irritability, muscle aches, muscle tension, nausea, nervous energy, rapid breathing, shortness of breath, sweating, trembling and twitching ... suppression of the immune system, digestive disorders, muscle tension, short-term memory loss, premature coronary artery disease, heart attack.

"In severe cases, when excessive worrying and high anxiety go untreated, they can lead to depression and even suicidal thoughts."[11]

A story is told that Death was walking toward a city one morning and a man asked, "What are you going to do?"
"I'm going to take a hundred people," Death replied.
"That's horrible!" the man said.
"That's the way it is," Death said. "That's what I do."
The man hurried to warn everyone about Death's plan. As evening fell, he met Death again. "You told me you were going to take hundred people," the man said. "Why did a thousand die?"
"I kept my word," Death responded. "I only took a hundred people. Worry took the others."[12]

How to Overcome Worry

Paul Taylor, at Eden Communications, gives a number of suggestions on how to overcome worry. The condensed list is given below:

- Get enough sleep. Sleep deprivation can increase anxiety.
- Many people are worried and anxious about events that will never actually happen to them ... Take life one day at a time.
- Do something that you enjoy to get your mind off your worries.
- Share your worries with a friend, relative, pastor or counselor.
- If there is something you can do to alleviate the problem, take action.
- Exercise can help lower anxiety. Regular brisk walks, running, swimming or other exercises can be a real stress reducer.[13]

Donna Clark Goodrich

No matter what may be the test,
God will take care of you.
Lean, weary one, upon His breast,
God will take care of you.

God will take care of you,
Thro' ev'ry day, O'er all the way.
He will take care of you;
God will take care of you.[15]

I Like to Worry

*I like to worry
It makes me feel
So important;
So fully master
Of my days
And destiny.
After all
If I don't
Fret
And fuss
And sputter
About things
Beyond my control
Who will?
If I don't
Keep God informed
About
What's going wrong
In His world
And how
He ought to handle it
How else
Will He know?
And how
Will He know
That I care?*

*I confess
I do have
A little trouble
With a few verses
In the Bible —
Put in by mistake
I'm sure
And totally
Irrelevant
Like 1 Peter 5:7
And Matthew 6:34.
I thought surely
Some later translator
Would leave them out.

But they haven't,
So I ignore them
And look
For important
Verses
That say
What I think
Ought to be said
Like Mark 13:33
— Especially
The watching.*

*Watching
All the things
That are going wrong
Makes it
Much easier
To worry.
Of course,
It takes up
A lot of the time
I could spend
Praying
But
If I'm
Going to shoulder
The responsibility
For things going
wrong
Anyhow,
Why pray
When I can worry?*

— Helen Temple

CHAPTER 12

LETTING GO OF DOUBT

Of course there's a God. Why would anyone doubt it? I had been taught that since early childhood, and I scorned those who denied His existence. But, as I grew older, suddenly doubt crept into my mind. Too many things had happened — not only the violent and criminal acts in the world around me — but in my own family: unexpected deaths, many surgeries and illnesses.

Where was God in all this? I wondered. I've always believed there is a God, but is there really? And, if so, how can I know for sure that what I've believed all these years is really true? Although I felt embarrassed, I admitted my doubts to a small group at a spiritual retreat. They prayed for me, and I continued to pray harder — that my head knowledge would travel again to my heart.

Then, one night, tossing and turning in bed because of a serious family crisis, I started praying. Without planning ahead what I would say, I said, "God, I know You're there. You've always been there." Of course! How could I not know there was a God? He had always been there for me in the past, and He would be with me now. At that moment, everything changed and all my doubt disappeared.

True faith goes into operation when there are no answers.
(Elizabeth Elliot)

What is doubt and why do we doubt? Kent Crockett says, "Doubts occur when what we expect to happen *isn't* happening, or what shouldn't be happening *is* happening. Circumstances are in direct conflict with what we believe. This causes us to be confused and waver between the two, wondering which is right."[1]

When Do We Doubt?

James A. Fowler says we doubt when:

- We don't know where God is taking us into the unknown and uncharted territory (think of Abraham who went out, not knowing where he was going).
- We don't know where this adventure will end.
- We don't know what God will do next.
- We don't know how God is going to work this out.
- We don't know when this situation will be settled.
- We don't know why God is allowing this circumstance or why God is acting as He does.[2]

A friend said that we also doubt because we judge the future by our past. But God's Word has a promise for those who doubt. James says, "If any of you lacks wisdom, he should ask God, who gives generously to all without finding fault, and it will be given to him." (James 1:5)

The devil had a closing down sale and was selling all his tools and devices of destruction. Someone asked him how much he wanted for the wedge of doubt. He said, "It's not for sale. I can get back into business with that anytime."

In the book of Mark, a father brought his son to Jesus to be healed of convulsions. Jesus said to him, "If thou canst believe, all things are possible to him that believeth."

The father replied, "Lord, I believe; help thou mine unbelief." (Mark 9:23-24 KJV)

Our pastor explained that passage this way: Lord, I believe *this* much (holding out his arms), but help me to believe this much (holding out his arms wider).

Lee Strobel, a Christian author, says,

"For many Christians, merely having doubts of any kind can be scary. They wonder whether their questions disqualify them from being a follower of Christ. They feel insecure because they're not sure whether it's permissible to express uncertainty about God, Jesus or the Bible. So they keep their questions to themselves — and inside, unanswered, they grow and fester and loom until they eventually succeed in choking out their faith."[3]

WHEN WE DOUBT THE EXISTENCE OF GOD

In sharing my doubting experience with friends, I discovered I wasn't the only Christian who had struggled with God's existence. Cass Wessel writes of her "aha" moment:

"Gnawing doubt tore through my childhood faith. Was God real? Did Jesus Christ really die to liberate humanity from their self-induced misery? Was the whole story a myth or was it true? If so, why did Jesus have to die? The questions swirled furiously through my mind.

"My husband and I were a team couple on an upcoming Marriage Encounter weekend, which forced me to look at my faith. In our team meeting, the lead minister assigned us the marriage and spirituality talk. We were to help other couples find spirituality in their own marriages. I objected, saying, 'Given all the heartache and viciousness in the world, I'm unsure God even exists. So how can I share about God in our marriage?'

"The minister answered me simply. 'Look for the good in your marriage and around you. There you will find God.'

"I shook my head. It couldn't be that simple. For one solid week, I searched for good memories. I argued with myself and an uncertain God. Even though I had an intellectual knowledge of Scripture and church teaching, were they right? What of the much-touted inconsistencies? Were my religion professors right, or my mother?

"At night, I tossed and turned. Nightmares disrupted my sleep. I became short-tempered with my children. Worse, I shut my husband out. How could he understand my doubt?

"Our next meeting was on a Thursday night. On Wednesday, I still doubted. That afternoon, I accused God of all sorts of inhumanity. I attacked the cross of Christ and His reputed resurrection. I shouted at my living room ceiling. 'It's not logical, not rational. It makes no sense.'

"I felt searing loneliness pierce my soul. Suddenly desolate, I started weeping and bolted for the kitchen to take refuge in a cup of coffee. As I sipped and sauntered back to the living room, a breeze caressed my face, though there were no open windows in our well-insulated house. I turned toward it, utterly exhausted. Cradling my cup of java in my hands, I prayed, 'God, I don't know if You are even real, but I'm tired of fighting. I still think the cross makes no sense, but I guess, if you say so … I guess, if You are God, then I am not, and You know more than I do. So I give in. Have it Your way.'

"That night, when I went to bed, I lay back on my pillow and closed my eyes. On the screen of my mind, Jesus Christ appeared bathed in glorious, golden light. Love shone from His eyes, embracing me. In that instant, I knew Scripture was true. Jesus is who He is claimed to be. He spoke two words into my mind, 'Follow me.' To this day, I fall to my knees and say, 'My LORD and my God.'"

When our son was in the sixth grade, he began questioning, "How do we know there's such a person called Jesus? No one's alive who has ever seen Him. All we know is what we read in the Bible."

During that time he was cast as Abraham Lincoln in a Thanksgiving Day program at school. Helping him learn his lines one day, I asked him, "How do we know there even is a person named Abraham Lincoln? No one's alive today who has ever seen him."

"It's in my history book," he replied. Then his face lit up. "I know what you're getting at," he said. "The Bible's more true than my history book, so we *can* know there really is a Jesus."

An atheist father was trying to prove to his daughter that there was no God. He wrote on a piece of paper: GOD IS NOWHERE!

"You're right, Daddy," the little girl exclaimed.

"What do you mean?" the father asked, confused.

"It's like my Sunday school teacher said: GOD IS NOW HERE!"

WHEN WE DOUBT IF THE BIBLE IS TRUE

G. Campbell Morgan had already enjoyed some success as a preacher by the time he was nineteen years old, but then he was attacked by doubts about the Bible. The writings of various scientists and agnostics disturbed him (e.g., Charles Darwin, John Tyndall, Thomas Huxley, and Herbert Spencer). As he read their books and listened to debates, Morgan became more and more perplexed. What did he do? He cancelled all preaching engagements, put all the books in a cupboard, locked the door, then went to the bookstore and bought a new Bible. He said to himself, "I am no longer sure that this is what my father claims it to be — the Word of God. But of this I am sure. If it be the Word of God, and if I come to it with an unprejudiced and open mind, it will bring assurance to my soul of itself."

The result? "That Bible found me!" said Morgan. The new assurance in 1883 gave him the motivation for his preaching and teaching ministry. He devoted himself to the study and preaching of God's Word.[4]

Years ago, I worked with a man who was a new Christian. One of his first goals was to read the Bible from beginning to end. "At first," he told me, "every time I had a question, I stopped to ask someone what it meant. Also," he said, "it seemed like I was finding contradictions that bothered me.

"Then," he added, "I decided to just write down the questions and keep reading." His face lit up. "And do you know, when I finished reading, all my questions had been answered."

Blaise Pascal says,

"If a single man had written a book foretelling the time and manner of Jesus' coming and Jesus had come in conformity with these prophecies, this would carry infinite weight. But there is much more here. There is a succession of men over a period of four-thousand years, coming consistently and invariably one after the other, to foretell the same coming; there is an entire people proclaiming it, existing for four-thousand years to testify in a body to the certainty they feel about it, from which they cannot be deflected by whatever threats and persecutions they may suffer. This is of a quite different order of importance."[5]

Even the disciple Peter had problems understanding the Bible. In his second epistle, speaking about the apostle Paul's writings, he says, "His letters contain some things that are hard to understand, which ignorant and unstable people distort, as they do the other Scriptures, to their own destruction." (2 Peter 3:16)

Do you have questions about particular events or verses in God's Word? Talk to Bible scholars, or look up those portions in a concordance or Bible encyclopedia. That will help you better understand the customs of those days.

When Illness Comes

Sometimes Christians feel that, because they have accepted Christ as their Savior and are attempting to live according to His commandments, they should be free from illness and other problems.

I've heard the story of the wise man and the foolish man since childhood, and often sang the chorus, "The wise man built his house upon a rock … The foolish man built his house upon the sand." But it took on new meaning a few years ago when our pastor preached on this Scripture, and pointed out that *the storms came upon both of them!* The difference in that story — and the difference in our lives — is that when the storms come, we have a firm foundation and our house doesn't have to fall.

On Christ, the solid Rock, I stand;
All other ground is sinking sand.[6]

The FREEDOM of *Letting Go*

When my mother was lying in a coma, Satan kept saying to me, "*If* there was a God, would your mother be like this today?" He reminded me of all the years she taught Sunday school, and was in church every time the doors were open.

Then one evening, standing by her bedside, my stepdad — an elderly man suffering from multi-infarct dementia — cleared his throat (as he always did when getting ready to ask me a question). "Donnie [his name for me], who made the world?"

"God did, Clarence," I answered.

He hesitated, and then asked, "Donnie, who made the sun?"

"God did," I repeated.

A few minutes later, "Donnie, who made the moon?"

What was this all leading to? I wondered, but answered, "God did."

Then it came again, "Donnie, who made the stars?"

Now, irritated, I replied, "God did, Clarence."

His face brightened and he said, "Then there must be a God somewhere!"

Yes, there was a God and He was in that room, especially several nights later when seventeen of my mother's children and grandchildren sang her favorite songs for an hour and a half, then each stepped up to her and told her what her life had meant to them. Although she lived two weeks after that, that was the night the family told her good-bye.

When Negative Things Come into Our Lives

If anyone had reason to doubt, it was Job. "This man was blameless and upright; he feared God and shunned evil." (Job 1:1) Yet, in one day, his oxen, donkeys, sheep, camels, and most of his servants were killed. As though that weren't enough, the same day, a wind struck the four corners of the house. It collapsed and he lost his sons and daughters.

What was his response? "Naked I came from my mother's womb, and naked I will depart. The LORD gave and the LORD has taken away; may the name of the LORD be praised." (Job 1:21) Not exactly the reaction I would have had.

Even though his wife and his friends told him to curse God and die, Job prayed for his friends, and "the LORD made him prosperous again and gave him twice as much as he had before."

I shared earlier in this book about the period after my mother died, and I went through several months of depression. It was difficult to read the Bible and it seemed my prayers hit a brick wall. Standing at the sink one day, doing dishes, my tears flowed almost as steadily as the water from the faucet. Finally, I shook my fist toward heaven and yelled, "Are you there, Lord? Is anyone even listening?" Suddenly, I heard these words from the television set in the living room, "The audio portion of our program is temporarily disrupted. Please stand by!"

If you're going through such a time right now, do not doubt that God is listening. He hasn't turned His back on you. As the old saying goes, "The answer may be 'yes,' 'no,' or 'wait awhile,' but He *will* answer."

Think back over some of the things you have prayed for in the past, and for which you're now thankful that God *didn't* answer the way you'd hoped He would. I'm thinking of several young men I dated whom I was sure were *the one,* but God led me to another man. I had also prayed for jobs I wasn't hired for, and later I saw God's wisdom in leading me to another position. He knows what is in your future and He will answer accordingly.

I love the words of the old hymn "If We Could See Beyond Today," especially the last verse:

If we could see, if we could know
We often say,
But God in love a veil doth throw
Across our way.
We cannot see what lies before,
And so we cling to Him the more,
He leads us till this life is o'er,
Trust and obey.[7]

When We Doubt If We're Christians

Although I love our denomination dearly (as I tell people, I first belonged to it by birth, and now by choice), it did have a lot of very strict rules. After every service, our pastor gave an invitation. Because so much of my friends' assurance of salvation was based on emotion rather than on certainty, every Sunday night found the same people at the altar — including me. Afterwards, when everyone finished praying, they sat on the front seat and we had testimonies, interspersed with choruses. (At that time, our evening service began at 7:30 and we often didn't get home until 10 p.m.)

My testimony usually went like this: "I thought I was a Christian, but realized during the week I wasn't. Now I know I am." A few weeks later, I would go to the altar again and give the same testimony.

I wrote earlier about the Monday night when I was in the eighth grade and did something I felt guilty about. It probably wasn't even anything that serious, but I recall thinking, "I don't want to wait until next Sunday to go to the altar," and I knelt by my bed and asked forgiveness. Not only did I feel peace after my prayer, but I realized I could talk to God *anytime* and He would answer.

Our faith journey is ongoing, with many starts and stops, sins and forgiveness. It doesn't mean we weren't Christians at the start.

It just means that we're growing as we should. Just as we know our mates better after years of marriage, we also come to a deeper relationship with Christ as we continue in our faith walk.

BIBLICAL PEOPLE WHO DOUBTED

One of the first patriarchs in the Bible who expressed doubt was Abraham. In Genesis 17, God said to him,

> *"I will bless [Sarah] and will surely give you a son by her. I will bless her so that she will be the mother of nations; kings of peoples will come from her."*
>
> *"Abraham fell facedown; he laughed and said to himself, 'Will a son be born to a man a hundred years old? Will Sarah bear a child at the age of 90?'" (17:16-17).*

Later, three men visited Abraham's tent and one of them said to him,

> *"'I will surely return to you about this time next year, and Sarah your wife will have a son.'*
>
> *"Now Sarah was listening at the entrance to the tent, which was behind him. Abraham and Sarah were already very old, and Sarah was past the age of childbearing. So Sarah laughed to herself as she thought, After I am worn out and my lord is old, will I now have this pleasure?*
>
> *"Then the Lord said to Abraham, 'Why did Sarah laugh and say, "Will I really have a child, now that I am old?" Is anything too hard for the Lord? I will return to you at the appointed time next year, and Sarah will have a son.'"*

The FREEDOM of *Letting Go*

> *"Sarah was afraid, so she lied and said, 'I did not laugh.'*
> *"But he said, 'Yes, you did laugh.'" (Genesis 18:10-15)*

If today, like Jeremiah, you're reaching out to a world that won't listen, God promises that He will restore and save you so you may serve Him.

In the New Testament, even John the Baptist doubted that Jesus — his own cousin — was the Messiah:

> *"After Jesus had finished instructing his twelve disciples, he went on from there to teach and preach in the towns of Galilee. When John, who was in prison, heard about the deeds of the Messiah, he sent his disciples to ask him, 'Are you the one who is to come, or should we expect someone else?'" (Matthew 11:1-3).*

And, of course, we couldn't conclude this chapter without mentioning the doubting disciple himself — Thomas.

> *"Now Thomas [also known as Didymus], one of the Twelve, was not with the disciples when Jesus came. So the other disciples told him, 'We have seen the Lord!'*
> *"But he said to them, 'Unless I see the nail marks in his hands and put my finger where the nails were, and put my hand into his side, I will not believe.'*
> *"A week later, his disciples were in the house again, and Thomas was with them. Though the doors were locked, Jesus came and stood among them and said, 'Peace be with you!' Then he said to Thomas, 'Put your finger here; see my hands. Reach out your hand and put it into my side. Stop doubting and believe.'"*
> *(John 20:24-27)*

Donna Clark Goodrich

Have you ever noticed in this story that in none of the New Testament accounts does it say that Thomas *actually put his hands in Christ's side?* It was enough for him that he *saw* the nail scars in His hand, and he exclaimed, "My Lord and my God!"

And, as one pastor said, "These are not the words of a doubter!"

CHAPTER 13

LETTING GO OF FEAR

According to Wikipedia, fear can be classified into two types: external and internal.

- *External fear* is caused by something outside of you, which you are strongly motivated to avoid; for example: fear of spiders.
- *Internal fear* is something inside of you that you link to a negative emotion; for example: fear developed out of low self-esteem.[1]

These fears can begin early in life. For example, many toddlers are afraid of the dark, sure that a monster is hiding under their bed or in their closets. Later, this fear can extend to separation anxiety when parents leave for work.

Television and movies have done a lot to create fear in children. For months, my then four-year-old granddaughter, Lindsay, had three imaginary playmates: Beebe, Coke, and Jan. They went everywhere with her, and her parents even had to save them seats at restaurants.

One day I realized I hadn't heard her talk about them in quite awhile, so I asked her, "What happened to Beebe, Coke, and Jan?"

"Oh," she answered nonchalantly, "they got killed in a drive-by shooting."

Researchers at Johns Hopkins University reported that, in 1960, the greatest fears of grade school children were: 1) animals,

2) being in a dark room, 3) high places, 4) strangers, 5) loud noises. In 1990, kids were afraid of the following: 1) divorce, 2) nuclear war, 3) cancer, 4) pollution, 5) being mugged.[2]

Many of these same fears continue on into the teen years, along with new ones. In a 2005 Gallup poll (U.S.A.), a national sample of adolescents between the ages of thirteen and fifteen were asked what they feared the most. The most frequently cited fear (mentioned by 8 percent of the teens) was terrorism. The top ten fears were, in order: terrorist attacks, spiders, death, being a failure, war, heights, criminal or gang violence, being alone, the future, and nuclear war.[3]

God doesn't want us to live our lives in constant fear. As Dr. E. Stanley Jones says,

> "I am inwardly fashioned for faith, not for fear. Fear is not my native land; faith is. I am so made that worry and anxiety are sand in the machinery of life; faith is the oil. I live better by faith and confidence than by fear, doubt and anxiety … We are inwardly constructed in nerve and tissue, brain cell and soul, for faith and not for fear. God made us that way."[4]

"Do not be afraid" appears three-hundred and sixty-five times in Scripture, one for each day of the year.

Some people suffer from Obsessive Compulsive Disorder (OCD), which involves repetitive actions such as excessive washing or cleaning, repeated checking, extreme hoarding, and opening and closing a door a certain number of times before entering or leaving a room. While these fears are unusual and may require counseling, other fears are more common, and we'll discuss some of them below. We'll also share the stories of people who have experienced

Fear of Losing Your Job

As mentioned in the chapter on worry, at the time of this writing, the national unemployment rate stands at almost 9 percent, with some states as high as 14 percent. To overcome this fear, you can do several things. One is to keep your résumé updated and be on the lookout for other opportunities, should the day come when you are laid off or your employer closes down.

Also, let your friends know. Networking is important in a job search. And, above all, pray and believe that God has your future in His hands. Matthew 10:31 says that you are worth more to God than many sparrows, and He cares for them. The songwriter tells us,

> Be still my soul; thy God doth undertake
> To guide the future as He has the past.[5]

Some people have used a layoff to go back to school or to realize their dream of opening their own business.

Paul Piotrowski says that one of the best ways to overcome the fear of losing your job is to constantly work on improving the value you provide to your employer, regardless of where you are working. Become so invaluable that your employer stays up at night worrying about losing you as an employee, not the other way around.[6]

Fear of Being Alone

Connie Peters experienced this fear:

> "Raised with four sisters and then marrying young, I had few occasions to stay home alone at night. However, when my

husband began working the night shift, I could hear every creak in the house and every rustle outside. Sometimes terror gripped me in such a way, I couldn't even think or pray. My kids were little and sensed when I was afraid. I didn't want them to become scared of staying in their rooms at night. I knew I needed God's help, and I began meditating on these scriptures:

'I lie down and sleep; I wake again, because the LORD sustains me. I will not fear though tens of thousands assail me on every side.' (Psalm 3:5-6)

'You will not fear the terror of night, nor the arrow that flies by day.' (Psalm 91:5)

'Do not fret because of evildoers or be envious of the wicked, for the evildoer has no future hope, and the lamp of the wicked will be snuffed out.' (Proverbs 24:19-20)

"As I meditated on these verses, the Lord worked a miracle in my heart and mind. Now I can spend the night alone and be at complete peace. At times, the fear does threaten to come back, but meditating on the verses again keeps it in check."

Jeanne Doyon also shared the same fear.

"When my children were very young (three under the age of two), my husband John would often be gone for two weeks at a time. I couldn't sleep. I would stay awake till midnight planning escape routes in case of fire or a burglar, even slept in a sweat suit to be ready for action if needed.

"Then, one night, the Lord spoke clearly in my spirit: 'Who is your protector, John or ME?' That was a turning point for me. I began searching the Word at night, and those times when John was away became times of growth as I began to see God as the One who watches over me. When I realized that everything that happens in our lives must first be sifted through His hands, I began to let go and allow Him to reign in all areas of my life.

"As my children grew older, I actually began enjoying the times my husband traveled. And as soon as this happened, his travel stopped. It was as if God said, 'You have learned well.'"

Fear of the Unknown

An Arab chief tells the story of a spy captured and sentenced to death by a general in the Persian army. This general gave the criminal a choice between the firing squad and "the big, black door."

As the moment for execution drew near, the general asked the spy, "What will it be, the firing squad or the big, black door?"

The spy hesitated, and then chose the firing squad. A few minutes after hearing the shots ring out, the general turned to his aide and said, "They always prefer the known to the unknown. People fear what they don't know. Freedom lies beyond the big door, but I've known only a few brave enough to make that choice."[7]

Shortly after my mother passed away, my stepdad came out to spend several months with us. In the advanced stages of multi-infarct dementia, he still enjoyed sharing a devotional time with us every morning, as he had done with my mother. One particular day the Scripture passage was from Romans 8:

"Who shall separate us from the love of Christ? Shall trouble or hardship or persecution or famine or nakedness or danger or sword? ... No, in all these things we are more than conquerors through him who loved us. For I am convinced that neither death nor life, neither angels nor demons, neither the present nor the future, nor any powers, neither height nor depth, nor anything else in all creation, will be able to separate us from the love of God that is in Christ Jesus our Lord." (Romans 8:31, 39)

Looking ahead to these verses, I thought, *He'll never understand all those big words. I'll skip them and just read verse 37:* "In all these things we are more than conquerors through him who loved us."

But something inside prompted me, *No, read ALL of them.*

When I finished, Clarence's face beamed and he said, "Nothing can separate us from God. That's nice!"

FEAR OF SPEAKING IN PUBLIC

Author and speaker Dell Smith Klein experienced this fear.

"Too shy to give an oral book report or read aloud in class, I was horrified to learn I would be required to take a speech class in order to graduate high school. My first day was a nightmare, but the instructor asked me to stay after class. As I wept, and for the first time talked about my fear (hands clammy, heart pounding), she suggested that I could stand behind a puppet stage. With her help, I worked out a creative way to give my first few speeches — a puppet show! My instructor interviewed me from outside the stage, the puppet answered and I became more emboldened with each 'speech.'

"As time went by, *I* interviewed the puppet and finally was able to give my final speech before the entire class with only four note cards and a puppet stage — and no lectern. Today, I speak at writing conferences, camp meetings, women's retreats, and churches — with no fear."

The FREEDOM of *Letting Go*

Paul Piotrowski, quoted above, suggests that one of the best ways to overcome this fear of speaking in public is:

" … to start really small and put yourself in a situation where you are in front of supportive, positive people. Prepare a presentation for just two of your friends over lunch. Then work on presenting to a group of your friends at your house, perhaps to five or six of your friends. Then maybe move up to something a bit bigger, like a presentation in front of a boardroom of people. Work your way up in baby steps and practice and prepare before your presentations. You may also want to join a Toastmasters group or some form of other public speaking group."[8]

FEAR OF FLYING

A missionary was preparing to leave for the field. Before she left, she scheduled a number of speaking engagements to raise money, which necessitated traveling about the country. This awakened her greatest fear — the fear of flying. In desperation, she asked the Lord for a Scripture verse to hang onto, and He gave her the following: "The eternal God is your refuge, and underneath are the everlasting arms." (Deuteronomy 33:27)

She said, from that day on, every time she boarded a plane, she envisioned it resting in the outstretched arms of God.

FEAR OF THE DARK

A mother and her four-year-old daughter were getting ready for bed. The child was afraid of the dark, but when the light was out, she caught a glimpse of the moon outside the window. "Mother," she asked, "is the moon God's light?"

"Yes," said the mother.

The next question was, "Will God put out His light and go to sleep?"

The mother replied, "No, my child. God never goes to sleep."

Then, out of the simplicity of a child's faith, the little girl said, "Well, so long as God is awake, I am not afraid."[9]

One night, when my husband was in the hospital, a storm raged outside our mobile home. As I climbed into bed, I could hear the wind whipping outside. "Well, Lord," I said, "here's where the rubber meets the road. Either You're going to take care of me, or You're not."

Tossing and turning for a while, I began to pray, and suddenly the words came to my mind: "I will lay me down in peace and sleep." I repeated them over and over, breathing in time with each word, and soon fell asleep. Each night he was gone, I went to sleep with that promise. (Eventually, I found the verse in Psalm 4:8: "I will lie down and sleep in peace, for you alone, O LORD, make me dwell in safety.") Proverbs 3:24 gives us the same assurance: "When you lie down, you will not be afraid; when you lie down, your sleep will be sweet."

Sometimes the Lord calms the storm. Sometime he lets the storm rage and calms his child.

Fear of Conflict in Relationships

Piotrowski says, "If you're out there living your life to the fullest, you will surely encounter situations where conflicts may arise. Don't avoid these situations. Just accept the fact that they will arise from time to time and you do have the ability to engage and negotiate a win-win resolution. Don't allow this fear to paralyze you into hiding from the world."[10]

The FREEDOM of *Letting Go*

Writer and speaker Adele Forrest shares an unnerving experience in her life and how God gave her victory.

"When a woman from my Bible study came to my home, attacked me and threatened my life, fear settled over me like a dark cloud. For weeks, the woman phoned my home and even walked up and down the street in front of my house, shouting curses at me, at God and the church. Another time, while I was away for several hours, she rearranged the lawn furniture and wrote strange words on the ground.

"Yet, Sunday after Sunday, she showed up at church, smiling and sweet. Everyone loved her. I couldn't avoid church since I was part of the worship team and I led the women's Bible study. And, certainly, I couldn't move to another location. Our new pastor was confused by what I told him had happened and what she told him about me. She refused to talk to him with me present.

"That dark cloud began to grow into a storm. I kept my window blinds drawn and the doors always closed. Friends learned to phone before visiting because I wouldn't answer the doorbell if my husband was away.

"Indeed, fear had taken serious hold of my life. I prayed for protection, pled the blood of Jesus and promised God I'd do anything for Him if only He'd keep that woman away from me.

"One night, when my husband was away overnight, I experienced terror. I turned out all the lights, except a nightlight in the front bathroom where I sat rocking between imagining this woman setting fire to my house and begging God for safety.

"For months before this young woman came into my life, I had been teaching a Bible class on Bible women who were unwavering in their faith. And now, I — the teacher — sat in a darkened bathroom terrified of a woman who might certainly destroy my life, but could not destroy my soul. In this time of terror, I realized the foolishness of my behavior. I thought, 'Am I a woman of God, or am I a wimp?' The question caused me to laugh. I switched on the bathroom light, ran into the hall and started turning on every light in the house.

"From a shelf in my bedroom closet, I pulled down a box of white fabric and took it back to my office. There I made a headband three and a half inches wide. On it, in black fabric marker, I wrote phrases and bits of scripture:

'I'm not afraid.' (Joel 1:21)

'He's ALL I need.'

'God, be in my head.'

'Peace John 14:27'

'PEACE'

'FEAR NOT'

My heart is NOT troubled.' (John 14:27)

'I am not afraid of night terrors or day arrows.' (Psalm 91:11)

"As I worked, that dark cloud of fear began to dissipate. Before the first ray of dawn, fear had fled.

"For the next three months, I wore that headband to church, to the grocery store, to the post office and when I went out for a walk. If I began to feel fear, I would stand in front of the mirror and read aloud the words of that headband. Every morning and night, I read verses from Scripture about peace and comfort, and began to meditate on Psalm 91.

"The harassment lasted another several months, but, with my 'coming out,' I no longer fell at the feet of fear, and over time, it grew less and less powerful in my life.

"The woman still lives in my town, but has changed to another church and simply ignores me if she sees me anywhere in town. And though I never plan to be friends with her again, I have forgiven her harassment and even gave her a nod of greeting one day at the post office."

Fear of Spiders

This is actually on the list of top ten fears. I once took a wolf spider to work in a jar so a friend could identify it, not knowing my supervisor was deathly afraid of them. She didn't know I had stashed it in the supply cabinet until she opened the door. But God can help us, even with this fear, as author Cass Wessel relates.

"As a child, I had an irrational fear of spiders. When I saw one spinning its delicate thread into a golden web, I would scream and run into the house, crying for my mother. This fear persisted well into adulthood and haunted me with every encounter.

"One evening at church, an older lady shared how she had overcome her irrational fears through prayer. Then she offered to pray for anyone stalked by fear. I got in line. After we prayed, she encouraged me to pray whenever fear arose.

"The next morning, I opened my eyes to see an eight-legged creature dangling over my face. I dared not scream and risk that it would drop into my open mouth. Instead, I scooted to the side and mentally prayed. Then I grabbed a paper tissue, captured it and dispatched it to wherever dead spiders go. Thereafter, every encounter was accompanied by prayer and less fear.

"These days, I love the way the morning dew glistens on their silken strands. I am also inclined to watch these critters weave their golden alchemy, and marvel at their skill and dexterity.

Then I praise God for having created such variety and beauty. (Having said as much, I doubt I will ever keep one as a pet.)

Fear of Losing a Loved One

Joan Perry's husband became a police officer a few months after they were married. "I worried all the time," she said. "At that time in his career, the Police Department was dealing with the Italian Mafia and they had even threatened our family, so these fears had overwhelmed me to the point of being sick. Finally, there came a point several years later, when my husband got called out, that I knelt at our fireplace in the middle of the night. I prayed for God to protect my husband and then remove my uncontrollable fears of losing him. That night, I placed my husband's life before Jesus' feet, and God rewarded me with a sense of peace."

Fear of Disease, Sickness or Poor Health

Sue Tornai fell at work one day, tripping over a cable on the floor. Embarrassed, she tried to get up. Her co-worker called 9-1-1, and her boss rode with her to the hospital. "It'll be okay," she smiled. Sue wanted to believe her, but didn't know whether she would walk again or be paralyzed.

The next morning, she underwent surgery during which the doctor repaired the broken femur by installing a titanium plate.

The night before, when her husband left the hospital, he asked what he could bring Sue the next day. In her pain and anxiety, she said, "Please bring my Bible." God's Word had sustained her for many years, and she knew it would give her strength to endure the days ahead. We'll let her tell the rest of the story:

"Four days after the surgery, the surgeon shook his head as he examined my hip. 'What's wrong?' I asked.

'Nothing,' he said softly. 'I just didn't expect this kind of healing.'

'You mean everything's okay?'

'Everything's great,' he laughed. 'You can go home today.'

"Back home, however, I thought about my future. Would I ever be able to walk without the walker? And if I did, would I have a limp? I worried about my appearance, and if I would embarrass my husband or children when they were with me. And I prayed — a lot.

"Four weeks later, my doctor released me to go back to work. I should have been happy with the fast healing; it was what we prayed for. Yet my joy was overshadowed with the anxiety of returning to the scene of the accident. I wasn't ready to leave the peaceful sanctuary of my home and move into the fast-paced work environment. I questioned if I could keep up and how my coworkers would accept me.

"I remember my reluctance getting into the driver's seat, and begging John to drive me to work the first day. He encouraged me to drive around the block, and if I was still afraid, then he would drive me. As I turned the key, I prayed for courage, and God reminded me of His love — the love I knew when I first believed, and the love I received from those who ministered to me through my disability. After the first stop sign, I crossed the street and God's love gave me the confidence I needed to keep driving. All my fears disappeared when I returned to work because He was with me.

"Today, I am aware that God's love worked in the people who shared in my healing and recovery: my coworkers, my family and friends who encouraged me, prayed for me, and brought over meals. Most of all, God's Word sustained me. He was with me through all the fears from my injury and my insecurities. His love accomplished the promise in 1 John 4:18, ' ... perfect love drives out fear ... '"

Some types of illness can be exacerbated by fear. Freelance writer Zillah Williams shares that she had been prone to periods of depression all her life. A few years ago she experienced the worst episode she had ever had. The basis of the depression: fear — fear and insecurity.

Then someone lent her copies of sermon notes from messages given by Canon Jim Glennon, who once led a healing ministry at St. Andrews Cathedral in Sydney, Australia. These sermons became a lifeline to Zillah as Canon Glennon had, himself, been a sufferer of fear and depression for most of his adult life, in fact. It was during that time that he heard God speak to him. Glennon said:

"I have only heard the voice of God about four or five times, and always at times of extreme need or difficulty. On this occasion, God said to me, 'Is there anything you can learn from all your problems?'

"That was the one thing I had not thought of. I could blame other people — which I did ... not a little. I understood my problems, but that didn't help. I could be filled with fear and depression, but I had never thought there was something I could learn ... [God] went on, 'You are to learn to depend on me more.'

"That changed my life!"...

Zillah said she then began to do as Canon Glennon suggested: to "pray without ceasing." (1 Thessalonians 5:17 KJV) She also began to repeat 2 Timothy 1:7 over and over: "For God hath not given us the spirit of fear, but of power, and of love, and of a sound mind." (KJV) Gradually, she recovered.

FEAR OF TERRORISM

What a beautiful promise Martin Luther gives us in the words of "A Mighty Fortress Is Our God":

> And though this world, with devils filled,
> Should threaten to undo us,
> We will not fear, for God has willed
> His truth to triumph through us.
> The prince of darkness grim —
> We tremble not for him;
> His rage we can endure,
> For lo! his doom is sure,
> One little word shall fell him.[10]

"In righteousness you shall be established; You shall be far from oppression, for you shall not fear; And from terror, for it shall not come near you." (Isaiah 54:14)

FEAR OF DEATH

A dear friend, in the last days of her battle with cancer, called me. "I'm not afraid to die," she told me. "I'm anxious to meet my Lord. It's just what I have to go through in the meantime."

I shared with her that the Lord promised to go with us, even in the *shadow* of death: "*Yea, though I walk through the valley of the shadow of death,* I will fear no evil; for thou art with me; thy rod and thy staff they comfort me." (Psalm 23:4-5 KJV, emphasis added) This was an encouraging thought to her.

Let me close with a personal experience. One of the fears I struggled with most of my life, has been the fear of death. It consumed my mind almost every day. It wasn't the fear of the unknown that bothered me; it was the verse in 1 Peter 4:18: "And if the righteous scarcely be saved, where shall the ungodly and the sinner appear." (KJV)

To me, the "righteous" were people like my mother and my godly Sunday school teacher. If they could "scarcely be saved," then what chance was there for me? At night I would lie in bed, thinking of all my failures and shortcomings, and worry that I wouldn't make it into God's kingdom.

One night, not so very long ago, I struggled with this fear again. Suddenly, I realized I was basing my salvation on *what I had done*, not *what Christ had done for me.* Looking at it from this point of view, I had a conversation with the Lord. It was as though He was asking me, "Did you ask me to forgive your sins?"

"Yes, Lord."

"And did I do it?"

"Yes, Lord."

"And have I brought them up against you again?"

"No, Lord."

"Then what is your worry?"

And for the first time in years, I fell asleep with peace in my heart!

CHAPTER 14

THE LAND BEYOND LETTING GO

At the present time, you may have no need to let go of everything described in this book. However, you may have dealt with one or more of these issues in the past — or perhaps you will in the future. And now that you have received help on letting go of these concerns, what next? Philippians 4:13 and 14 says, "Forgetting what is behind … *I press forward.*" It's like riding a bicycle. You can't just put your feet on the pedals and sit there without the bike falling over. You have to choose which way to go. So where do you go from here?

You've found closure after the death of a loved one. Can you now pick up the pieces and go on with your life?

You've let go of a failure. Have you found the courage to try again?

You've quit hanging on to the successes of the past. Will you now give God credit for the gifts He has loaned you?

You've cut up your credit cards. Have you now set up a budget and made plans to begin living within your income, realizing that possessions do not bring happiness?

You've put hurtful words and actions in the "forgiven" file. Will you forbid them to play over and over in your mind like a broken record?

Your children have left the nest. Can you now let them live their own lives, and begin doing some of the things you've always wanted to do?

Even though you may have some health issues, will you now put them in the hands of the Great Physician and let Him give you strength for those rough days?

You've considered the alternative to growing old. Now can you start enjoying the senior discounts and not let the AARP letters bother you?

You've taken all your past sins to the cross. Can you also leave the guilt there?

Now that you've let go of always wanting to be in control, can you accept that God is in control and He does a much better job?

And have you decided not to let worry, doubt, and fear take over your life, believing that God has your future in His hands?

Luke 11 tells of an evil spirit that came out of a man. It looked for rest and couldn't find it, so it returned to the house it left. "When it arrives, it finds the house swept clean and put in order. Then it goes and takes seven other spirits more wicked than itself, and they go in and live there. And the final condition of that man is worse than the first." (vs. 25-26)

That won't be your story if you find something positive to replace the negatives you've let go of in your life.

The following passage helped me after my mother died. "Now after the death of Moses ... it came to pass that the LORD spoke unto Joshua ... saying, Moses, my servant is dead; now therefore arise." (Joshua 1:2-3) These verses showed me that God didn't want me to stay in my grief; He wanted me to arise and continue the work He had given my mother to do. And just as God's promises to Moses held fast for Joshua, so too the promises He had given my mother during her long walk with Him would keep me steady.

God tells us not to "call to mind the former things, or ponder things of the past." He says He will do something new in our lives.

The FREEDOM of *Letting Go*

Now that we've laid aside "every weight" (Hebrews 12:1), we can run the race set before us.

Adam Clarke suggests that this "weight" alludes to the long garments worn in the eastern countries, which, if not laid aside or tucked up in the girdle, prevented a man from running a race. As those who ran in the Olympic races threw aside everything that might impede them in their course, so we must throw aside anything that might hinder us in our Christian race.

What are these weights for you? Perhaps they are the things we've mentioned in this book: grief, failure, success, possessions, hurts, children, health, youth, guilt, craving control, worry, doubt, and fear. Hanging on to even one of these can hinder us in our race.

> He breaks the pow'r of canceled sin;
> He sets the pris'ner free.[1]

In his book, *Crave,* talking about bondage (his book deals specifically with food), Chris Tomlinson says, "When you finally break free from your bondage to food, realize that you will likely need 'replacement therapy.' Because it has long been second nature for you to use food as an emotional 'go-to,' many of you will be heading off into this free, new world feeling somewhat vacant and uncertain."

He says, now that you have unloaded your "emotional baggage," you'll need to learn what to pack for a healthy life journey.[2]

You may be feeling that right now. You've leaned on the crutches of grief or failure or guilt for so long; now that you're experiencing the freedom of letting go, you're wondering what can take their place. Tomlinson says that, "The security of bondage can often seem easier than the anxiety of freedom."[3]

Our pastor agrees. He says it may be scary to go with God into the unknown future, but it's better than staying where you are — alone.

> Wherever He may guide me,
> No want shall turn me back;
> My Shepherd is beside me,
> And nothing can I lack.
> His wisdom ever waketh;
> His sight is never dim.
> He knows the way He taketh,
> And I will walk with Him.[4]

Esther Eddy Hunt tells a beautiful story of moving into a new house blessed with the only tree in the neighborhood — a graceful red ash located in the center of their backyard, giving shade all day. The children and friends played around, climbed it, and hid behind it during games of hide-and-seek. Birds and squirrels also found a home in it.

Eventually, the children left. Two years before Hunt's husband died, they were advised to cut down the now dying tree. Her husband couldn't bear to do it, so they allowed it to stand. After he died, Hunt finally consulted two men who said, "Let it go now for the remaining live wood, or face a costly cutting."

On the day chosen, Hunt deliberately chose not to be at home. She returned after dark. Trembling, she took a small flashlight and crept out into her back yard. There at her feet lay the towering friend, awaiting the woodman's saw. With great sadness, she went back into the house.

The next morning, at daybreak, she awoke and hurried to the window to look at the "corpse" once again. But wonder of wonders:

The FREEDOM of *Letting Go*

"The sight I saw," she writes, "was a glimpse of heaven, for the cutting of our tree had opened up a previously unseen and more beautiful view of trees beyond."[5]

What trees do you have in the back yard of your life that you haven't wanted to cut down? Perhaps you insist they have given you shade, but what beautiful views are they hiding that God wants you to see?

*****

You can find such freedom in letting go, such joy in looking toward the future. "Forgetting those things which are behind, I press forward." Won't you join me?

END NOTES

INTRODUCTION

1 Norman Vincent Peale, *A Guide to Confident Living* (Englewood Cliffs, NJ: Prentice-Hall, Inc., 1948), 123.

2 Audrey Menen in *House & Garden,* quoted in *Reader's Digest,* January 1972, 155.

3 Barbara Bartocci, "Let Go and Live," *Reader's Digest,* October 1989, 103-06.

4 Author Unknown.

5 Fr. Robert Gehring, Maryknoll Associate Priest from the Diocese of Gary, Indiana, serving in Bolivia. Accessed August 4, 2011 at http://www.latter-rain.net/articles/co-dependency.html

CHAPTER 1
Letting Go of Grief

1 Mark Metcalf, "Good Grief," *Herald of Holiness,* September 1997, 35.

2,3,4 Doug Manning, Don't Take My Grief Away (San Francisco: Harper & Row, Publishers, 1984), 41. This book was reprinted in a Third Edition, *Don't Take My Grief Away From Me,* by In-Sight Books, Oklahoma City, OK, 2011.

5 John Henry Jowett, *My Daily Meditation* (Pasadena, CA: First Church of the Nazarene, republished 1983).

6 Manning, op. cit.
7 Cindy Herf, "Time to Let Go." Used by permission.
8 Ann Womack Lundberg, "Beauty for Ashes," *Herald of Holiness,* June 15, 1988, 15.
9 Leona Choy, *Singled Out For God's Assignment* (paraphrase from book review) (Winchester, VA: Golden Morning Publishing, 1996).
10 "In God's Own Time," Dave Clark. ©1984. Emmanuel Music (ASCAP). All rights reserved and controlled by Ben Speer Music. Used by permission.
11 "The Ship," by Victor Hugo.

CHAPTER 2
Letting Go of Failures — Your Own and Other People's

1 John Snider, "When Your Life Falls Flat…Lift Your Spirit With These Hopeful Words," *Today's Christian Woman,* Fall 1981, 74-75. This article first appeared on Kyria.com. Used by permission of Christianity Today International, Carol Stream, IL 60188.
2 Ibid., 76.
3 Gordon Chilvers, "Don't Accept Failure As Final," *Herald of Holiness,* March 15, 1981, 8.
4 http://www.disneydreamer.com/Pin.htm
5 David G. Rogne, Sermons for Sundays After Pentecost. Illustrations@CLERGY.net.
6 Snider, 72.
7 http://www.disneydreamer.com/Pin.htm
8 M.H. Schubert, *Guideposts* magazine, October 1974, 21.
9 Snider, 76.
10 Wightman Weese, *Back in Touch* (Wheaton, IL: Tyndale House Publishers, Inc., 1987), 10.

11 Audrey J. Williamson, *Far Above Rubies* (Kansas City, MO: Beacon Hill Press, 1961), p. 65.
12 http://sidsavara.com/personal-development/famous-failures-michael-jordan-abraham-lincoln-and-jk-rowling
13 Quoted in Joe G. Emerson, *I Wanted the Elevator, But I Got the Shaft* (Nashville, TN: Dimensions for Living, 1993), 92.
14 Robert H. Schuller, *You Can Become the Person You Want to Be* (New York: Hawthorn Books, 1973), 73.
15 Dave Clark, "He Covered My Scars with Love," ©1979 Emmanuel Music ASCAP. Used by permission.

CHAPTER 3
Letting Go of Successes

1 Hannah Whitall Smith, *The Christian's Secret of a Happy Life* (New York: Fleming Revell, 1870), 145.
2 *Jesus and the Intellectual,* Written by Bill Bright ©2003. Bright Media Foundation and Campus Crusade for Christ Inc. Formerly ©1959-2003 Campus Crusade for Christ, Inc. All rights reserved. No part of the work may be changed in any way or reproduced or stored in any form without written permission from Bright Media Foundation and Campus Crusade for Christ, Inc.
3 Bob Phillips, *42 Days to Feeling Great* (Eugene, OR: Harvest House Publishers, 2001), 43
4 J. Carl Laney, *Everything I Know About Success I Learned from the Bible* (Grand Rapids, MI: Kregel Publications, 1996), 146.
5 Dave Clark, "Put Your Dream Where Your Heart Is" ©1987 John T. Benson/ASCAP, Used by permission.

CHAPTER 4
LETTING GO OF POSSESSIONS

1 Rick and Bonnie Ryding, "Enough Is Enough." *Holiness Today,* November 2007, 6-7.
2 Marjorie Holmes, "A Woman's Conversation with God," *Woman's Day* magazine, March 1974.
3 Dave Donaldson, *The Compassion Revolution* (Eugene, OR: Harvest House Publishers, 2010), 144.
4 http://www.real-estate-online.com/articles/art-380.html. Accessed June 20, 2011.
5 Amy Bjork Harris and Thomas A. Harris, *Staying OK* (New York: Harper & Row, Publishers, 1985), 239.
6 *Daily Bread,* August 16, 1988.

CHAPTER 5
LETTING GO OF THE HURTS IN YOUR LIFE

1 Lynda Dallyn, "Forgiving first step to freedom," *Arizona Republic, SE Valley Living,* September 9, 2009, 211.
2 Stan Toler and Martha Bolton, *God Has Never Failed Me, But He Sure Has Scared Me to Death a Few Times!* (Tulsa, OK: Honor Books, 1998), 128.
3 Jean Harder, *Bound by Unforgiveness* (Phoenix, AZ: Debora House Ministries, 1983), 3.
4 Kitty Chappell, I *Can Forgive If I Want To — Forgiving the Unforgivable.* Published by Vocatio Publishers, Poland. Limited copies available in English at: www.kittychappell.com. Updated and revised version pending release by Tate Publishers.
5 Bill and Pam Farrel, *Every Marriage Is a Fixer-Upper* (Eugene,

OR: Harvest House Publishers, 2005), 94.
6 http://jmm.aaa.net.au.articles/9937.htm.
7 Malcolm Smith, *Forgiveness* (Tulsa, OK: Pillar, 1992), 6-7.
8 June Hunt, *Keeping Your Cool… When Your Anger Is Hot!* (Eugene, OR: Harvest House Publishers, 2009), 192.

CHAPTER 6
LETTING GO OF YOUR CHILDREN

1 Marian Edelman Borden, "Old Enough to Know Better." *Clarity,* April/May 2000, 61.
2 Lysa TerKeurst, *Am I Messing Up My Kids?* (Eugene, OR: Harvest House Publishers, 2010), 99.
3 Max Lucado, *Six Hours One Friday* (Portland, OR: Multnomah Books, 1989), 47-8.
4 C. Roy Angell, *Iron Shoes* (Nashville: Broadman Press, 1953), 56.
5 Guy Greenfield, *The Wounded Parent — Coping with Parental Discouragement* (Grand Rapids: Baker Book House, 1982), 11, 23, 67.
6 Pam Farrel, *The Treasure Inside Your Child* (Eugene, OR: Harvest House Publishers, 2001), p. 6.

CHAPTER 7
LETTING GO OF HEALTH ISSUES

1 E-mail newsletter from Janet Paschal, August 26, 2005. Used by permission.
2 Marion H. Nelson, M.D., *Why Christians Crack Up* (Chicago, Moody Press, 1967).
3 Wesley Tracy, "Disappointment with God," *Herald of Holiness,* August 1989, 2.

4 You can read Cindy's story in her book *A Heart Like Mine* (Eumenclaw, WA: WinePress Publishing Group, 2009), or visit her Web site at http://www.aHeartLikeMine.com.
5 Jill Briscoe, *There's a Snake in My Garden* (Grand Rapids, MI: Zondervan, 2975), 21.
6 John Ruskin, http://allsaintsthomasville.org/page/304/273.
7 "When a Brick Spawned a Book," *Our Daily Bread,* March 18, 1980.
8 George Matheson, http://www.moreillustrations.com/Illustrations/sorrow%206.html
9 C. Austin Miles, "In the Garden."
10 George L. Smith, "God's Good Intentions," *Come Ye Apart,* July 2, 2001.
11 Marlene Bagnull, "Sensitivity," *Standard,* May 9, 1982, 7.
12 Stuart and Jill Briscoe, "When God Says 'NO'." *Charisma,* June 1987, 13.
13 Dave Clark, "I've Been There." ©1986 Emmanuel Music/ASCAP. All rights reserved. Used by permission. (Read Dave's story in *Healing in God's Time* (Donna Clark Goodrich [Washington, DC: Believe Books, 2009]).

CHAPTER 8
Letting Go of Your Youth

1 http://thejokes.co.uk/miscellaneous-jokes-7.php
2 E. Stanley Jones, *Christian Maturity.* Quoted in Henry Gariepy, *Light in a Dark Place* (Wheaton, IL: Victor Books, 1965), 73.
3 Joanne Bailey Baxter, http://nitewriter.net/whenimanoldlady.htm.

CHAPTER 9
LETTING GO OF GUILT

1 Norman Vincent Peale, *A Guide to Confident Living* (Englewood Cliffs, NJ: Prentice-Hall, Inc., 1948), 41.

2 Philip Yancey and Tim Stafford, *Unhappy Secrets of the Christian Life* (Grand Rapids, MI: Zondervan Publishing House, ©1979 by Youth for Christ International), 51.

3 Quoted in Neil Anderson, *Breaking the Bondage of Legalism*, (Eugene, OR: Harvest House Publishers, 2003), 68.

4 Pat Springle, *Codependency: Breaking Free from the Hurt and Manipulation of Dysfunctional Relationships* (Nashville, TN: LifeWay Press, 1993), 90.

5 Corrie ten Boom, *Tramp for the Lord* (Fort Washington, PA: Christian Literature Crusade, 1974), 179.

6 Peale, 37.

7 Harold J. Sala, *Making Your Emotions Work for You* (Eugene, OR: Harvest House Publishers, 1996/2009), 100.

8 "It Is Well with My Soul," Horatio G. Spafford, 1828–1888. (emphasis added)

9 David Eckman, *Becoming Who God Intended* (Eugene, OR: Harvest House Publishers, 2005), 153.

CHAPTER 10
LETTING GO OF CONTROL

1 Michele Pullia Turk, "Why we're a nation of 'control freaks'," *USA Weekend*, January 16-18, 1998, 10.

2 Dean Nelson, "The Enthroned King," *Come Ye Apart* devotional booklet (Kansas City, MO: Nazarene Publishing House), April 11, 1984.

3 Lisa Bevere, *Out of Control and Loving It* (Orlando, FL: Creation House, 2006), ix-x.

4 Leslie Williams, "Who's in Control?", *Standard,* March 21, 1999, 6-7.

5 Cindy Valenti-Scinto, *A Heart Like Mine* (Enumclaw, WA: WinePress Publishing Group, 2009), 152-53.

6 Scinto, 150-51.

7 Michael B. Ross, *Come Ye Apart,* December 28, 1980.

8 Dave Clark, "He's All I Cannot Be," ©Emmanuel Music (ASCAP). All rights reserved and controlled by Ben Speer Music, P.O. Box 40102, Nashville, TN 37204. International copyright secured. Made in U.S.A.

9 Elisabeth Elliott, *The Path of Loneliness* (Nashville, TN: Thomas Nelson Publishers, 1988), 134.

CHAPTER 11
Letting Go of Worry

1 James A. Fowler, ©1999. http://www.christinyou.net/pages/worry.html

2 http://en.wikipedia.org/wiki/Worry_doll

3 http://en.wikipedia.org/wiki/Kombol%C3%B3i

4 www.ctc.uidaho.edu/default.aspx?pid=64768 (University of Idaho Counseling & Testing Center)

5 "Overheard in An Orchard," Elizabeth Cheney

6 John Newton, English author and composer, 1725–1807.

7 David Roth, pastor of New Church of Boulder Valley, Colorado. "Live with Less Anxiety and More Joy." http://www.newchurch.org/connection/issues/dealing-with-fear-and-worry/live-with-less-anxiety-blog.html

8 Ira Stanphill, "I Know Who Holds Tomorrow," ©1950 by Singspiration, Inc. All rights reserved.
9 Dale Carnegie, *How to Stop Worrying and Start Living* (New York: Pocket Books, Div. of Simon & Schuster, Inc., 1948), 1.
10 "Lead, Kindly Light," John H. Newman, 1801–1890
11 WebMD: www.webmd.com/balance/how-worrying-affects-your-body?print=true
12 http://www.infocera.com/THE_POWER_OF_WORRYING_1382.htm
13 Paul Taylor, Eden Communications, 2001. http://www.christiananswers.net/q-eden/anxiety.html
14 "God Will Take Care of You," Cavilla D. Martin, 1869–1948.

CHAPTER 12
Letting Go of Doubt

1 Kent Crockett, *The 911 Handbook* (Peabody, MA: Hendrickson Publishers, 2003), 16.
2 James A. Fowler @ http://www.christinyou.net/pages/doubt.html.
3 Lee Strobel, found at http://www.heritagechurchmuskego.org/sermons/oct08/10.5.2008.pdf.
4 *Wycliffe Handbook of Preaching & Preachers* (Chicago: Moody Press, 1984), 211.
5 Blaise Pascal, *Pensees,* 332.
6 "The Solid Rock," Edward Mote, 1797–1874
7 Norman Clayton, "If We Could See Beyond Today." Copyright 1943 in "Word of Life Melodies #1" by Norman J. Clayton. Assigned to Norman Clayton Publishing Co. ©Renewed 1971, Norman Clayton Publishing Co., owner.

CHAPTER 13
LETTING GO OF FEAR

1 http://en.wikipedia.org/wiki/Fear
2 *Back to the Bible Today,* Summer, 1990, 5.
3 Ibid.
4 www.sermonillustrations.com/a-z/fear.htm
5 "Be Still My Soul," Katharina von Schlegel, 1697–1768
6 http://www.paulymath.com/2008/04/23/14-most-common-fears-in-life-and-what-to-do-about-them/
7 Leonard Sweet, *1001 Quotes, Illustrations, and Humorous Stories for Preachers, Teachers, and Writers* (Grand Rapids, MI: Baker Books, 2006), 402.
8 http://www.paulymath
9 http://www.moreillustrations.com/Illustrations/fear%201.html
10 "A Mighty Fortress Is Our God," Martin Luther, 1483–1546

CHAPTER 14
THE LAND BEYOND LETTING GO

1 "O For a Thousand Tongues to Sing," Charles Wesley, 1707–1788.
2 Chris Tomlinson, *Crave* (Eugene, OR: Harvest House Publishers, 2110), 121.
3 Tomlinson, 172.
4 "In Heavenly Love Abiding," Anna L. Waring, 1823–1910.
5 Esther Eddy Hunt, "The Tree and I," *Herald of Holiness,* November 15, 1984, 18.

CPSIA information can be obtained at www.ICGtesting.com
Printed in the USA
LVOW06122011O412

277138LV00001B/4/P